Children in Play

Barry Nicholson

Children in Play

First paperback edition published 2020.

A catalogue record for this book is available from the British Library.

ISBN: 9780993243875

Published by Starhands Publishing UK (subsidiary of Nicholson International)

Printed in the United States

DAVOS
SKOLSTREJK
FÖR
KLIMATET

CONTENTS

Contents
List of Play Scripts

References
About the Author
From the Same Author

LIST OF PLAY SCRIPTS

Introduction

Welcome!

Do you know any famous children? Greta Thunberg, Dick Whittington, Sky Brown, Harry Potter and many more. Here they are in play! Each unit gives a short description of the youngster followed by a play script designed to enliven your classroom or community centre. Your students will enjoy acting out the plays and will wake up to the joys of practical drama and literature.

Plays and Stories

A play, in a theatrical sense, is a piece of writing intended to be acted in a theatre or similar place of performance; it is a dramatic work for stage or to be broadcast. An intriguing alternative definition sees 'play' as a light or brisk, constantly changing movement, as in 'a play of light'; or on an even higher level as freedom of action or activity, as in 'a full play of the mind'. Whereas I do not expect our students to encounter this higher state of being, it would, however, be nice if their creative juices were squeezed and stretched a little.

We often ask our students to write a story or order a sequence of events so that they make sense, and we usually use the past simple to achieve this. Essentially, a 'story' is a narrative, either true of fictional, designed to interest, amuse, or instruct the reader; and this is often a connected series of events that can be either true or imagined.

Related to this is a 'skit': a satirical or humorous story or sketch, especially one done by amateurs. It derives from the word 'sketch', and is often a comedic segment of a show or performance that often makes a joke of something. Certainly this element of humour is a theme that crops up throughout this book, and your children or teens will no doubt be eager to tap in to this valuable way of viewing the world at large.

The definitions suggest some kind of public performance, for example on TV or radio. Though I realise this is beyond the capability of most of us in the classroom or community centre, it may be possible to experiment with a video camera or other audio-visual recording device as resources and technology allow. Failing that, a well-rehearsed public performance will certainly do!

Scope and style

This book is primarily aimed at parents, teachers, and youth community leaders and their child or children, but there is also much of interest to the general reader. The stories and skits are written in a simple and enjoyable way, but do not patronise the reader or student.

Thankfully English is an art, not a science; it is descriptive rather than prescriptive; it is a creative and cultural act. Throughout, the English language is taken as a creative being; an abstract entity that can be neither seen nor heard except in its manifestation as the written word or spoken utterance. This is expressed no more so than in a short play or skit. And, as Shakespeare would have it, "all the world's a stage, and all the men and women mere players" ('As You Like It' Act II Scene VII).

I want to motivate and inspire – that means teachers, parents and youth leaders as well as children and teens – and it is in this light that this book has been written. Though it does not claim to be *the* answer, or even *an* answer, the book does claim to be a *way*, a way to approach your lessons or study period through literature, stories and drama.

The real question is one of motivation, of getting students motivated to study, and to help them help their peers to success too. The skills our youngsters get in these early days will help propel them into the future – their future – towards high school, university and beyond. As they progress through time, the study skills, methods and motivation techniques we show them now will stick with them and be added to and developed by them; education, drama and story-telling skills that will stay with and guide them, that they themselves can pass on to others.

Students can then progress in their studies with a sense of purpose and confidence.

Structure and Layout

Each unit follows the same basic pattern. After the title there is a short summary of the story called 'In Brief'. Here, the story is told, mostly in past simple and in prose. It is designed to be read either in one's head or out loud, perhaps before an audience or class of students in assembly.

Then the play script itself. First there is a list of characters that appear in the play – some are human, some animals, and some things. Then the setting is given, which gives ideas for scenery; then the script. I have tried to keep stage directions to a minimum or, in some circumstances not at all, when directions are obvious and so obsolete. The 'Director's Corner' gives further suggestions for the set, costumes, props, lighting and sound (see the section below).

As a parent, teacher or youth leader, it is your creative juices that are equally as important as the children's, and so you should feel free to adapt or add to the presented materials if you judge it to be correct, according to your opinion, resources, and working environment.

The Stories

The stories are divided into four sections:

- ❖ Children Today
- ❖ Kings, Queens and Rulers
- ❖ Fairy Tales and Fantasy
- ❖ It Really happened

Each theme presents four stories (and following them, four plays). The sixteen units are:

1. Greta Thunberg
    Has been campaigning for the environment;

2. Sky Brown
    An ambitious pre-teen skateboarder;

3. Coco Gauff
    Upcoming tennis star who triumphed at Wimbledon;

4. Billie Eilish and Justin Bieber
    Two of the bad guys of modern pop;

5. Julius Caesar

His youth, ambition and power led to his bloody demise;

6. King Tut
   The world's most famous pharaoh;

7. Pocahontas
   A symbol of bringing Native Americans and colonials together;

8. Dick Whittington
   He turned again to become Lord Mayor of London;

9. Harry Potter
   Harry, Ron and Hermione are off on adventures again;

10. Huckleberry Finn
    Whose story portrays life in nineteenth century Missouri;

11. Peter Pan
    One night Peter asks the children to join him in Neverland;

12. Charlie and the Chocolate Factory
    An odd bunch went to visit Wonka's chocolate factory;

13. Peter the Wild Boy
    A boy found in the forest who became 'civilised';

14. Pablo Picasso
    Who could draw before he could talk;

15. Amadeus Mozart
    Could play and compose music from a very early age;

16. Before the Beatles
    A lot happened in the few years before the Beatles.

The Props & Costume Box

Children and teens have great imagination and, at this level, simple props and costumes will do. For our purposes, the 'props box' and 'costume box' are one and the same.

Props are an essential part of any staged performance, and can be elaborate and complicated or as simple as a table and chair. Usually a skit or short play designed for (or written by) children or teens will veer towards the latter, making use of whatever is in the classroom or community centre. That is not to say that a few well-chosen and placed props would not enhance the performance. Think plastic daggers and tomato ketchup for a murder-mystery, for example.

Sharman (2004) defines a 'prop' as "practically everything on the set that is not nailed down – from the pictures on the walls to the contents of a handbag", which can be divided into the following categories: furniture (tables, chairs), glass and pottery (bottles, pots), food and drink (both real and fake), flowers and plants, personal props (like the contents of a handbag). To which I add : classroom-related (desks, bags, whiteboard), breakable or broken (that may be broken as part of the script, like a jug thrown to the floor), intellectual (things spoken about but not seen), people as props (like children dressed as trees in the background), wearable (a pair of glasses, a wig).

Let's move on to the 'costume' part of the box. At this level simple costumes, often just one or two fancy dressing-up clothes, will do. The question of make-up will probably not arise at all. So, keep it simple – the simpler the better – and remember that you only have to *suggest* a character by their appearance: you're not going for a Hollywood Oscar.

For our purposes the prop box and costume box are combined. I'd recommend you get an old (large) cardboard box from the local supermarket, or arrange all the bits and bobs on a table (as Sharman suggests). I prefer a large cardboard box because it is portable and introduces an element of 'lucky dip'.

Lighting and Sound Effects

Lighting, in a short children or teen's play performed in front of peers, may not be a consideration. But a few of the plays presented in this book could do with a sprinkle of lighting effects so to enhance dramatic effect. And I am not anticipating that your students will use sound effects other than the very simplest. Some of the plays involve several scenes, and the gaps between them (when costumes and furniture are being changed) could be filled with interlude music. But sound effects for our purposes are a luxury, not a necessity.

The Director's Corner

The 'Director' could either be you, as the student's mentor, teacher, or community group leader, or it could be one of the students themselves. If students are to work in small groups and write and produce their own play or skit then the role of the director is far less important. On the other hand, if there is to be a final performance in front of parents and/or peers, then the choice of a confident director who can, literally, direct, becomes paramount. I think that within the scope of this book, it can be assumed that the 'adult' will be named the director.

So what kind of things does a director do? Essentially, they plan the whole thing from start to finish, from choosing who plays what part, to saying who stands or moves where on stage. This is not to say that the children or teens will have no say in anything – on the contrary, it is partially the director's role to listen to and incorporate ideas and suggestions if they are appropriate. Have a think about the props and costume box, the lighting and sound effects, the set design, and also matters such as getting everyone in the right place at the right time, someone falling ill and not being able to take part, or a change of classroom or venue at the last moment. These are all the responsibility of the director. The director must have a firm overview of proceedings and a clear idea of 'the big picture'.

It depends on your circumstances, of course, but sometimes the students can be set up in small groups of, say, four or five, and told to get on with it by themselves. It is a good idea in this case to give the students some guidance as to how to go about the task, maybe a printed handout with a sequence of things to do: name of the play, character list, who is to be set and scenery manager, costume designer, script writer, and so on. It is a good idea for the group to elect a 'group leader' from the outset – a kind of pseudo-director.

Whoever is directing, or leading, someone will have to come up with some sort of a basic set. I'm not suggesting lavish backdrops lit with super-troopers and glitterballs (can you imagine?) – a table and chair will do. You might like to put up some cardboard hills behind Dick Whittington, or some trees behind Peter the Wild Boy, for example. Keep it simple, and remember that what the audience can see from the pits is less defined compared to what you can all see on stage!

Moving Forward

There are lots of opportunities to get out and about with your students. Most of the stories in this book can be tied to a geographical location, and it makes sense to plan your excursion according to topic. These visits will have the effect that the stories and plays come to life!

What more can I say? Enjoy this collection of stories and plays, and all things considered your children and teens will enjoy them too.

Barry Nicholson
London 2020

How Dare You! The Greta Effect

In Brief

Wildfires in eastern Australia, Venice flooded and underwater, the polar caps melting… the world's climate is in crisis, and straight-speaking Greta Thunberg has been campaigning to help the environment since 2018.

Her voice has become so powerful that there is even a 'Greta Effect' to describe her impact on the world stage. Greta likes to talk in soundbites; "How dare you!" is a famous line from her 2019 United Nations speech; "You haven't seen anything yet" is a more recent example (January 2020). Famously she has had spats with Donald Trump who has mocked her "anger management problem" with the tweet "Chill Greta, chill!" Nonetheless she won 'Time Person of the Year 2019', has published a book 'No One Is Too Small to make a Difference', and has been nominated for the Nobel Peace Prize. Most importantly she has inspired and empowered a whole new generation of climate-conscious teens.

Greta Thunberg was born on 3rd January 2003 in Stockholm, Sweden. She first heard about climate change in 2011 (aged 8) and couldn't understand why so little was being done about it. She became ill with the thought of it; she lost weight and stopped eating and talking for a while. She was diagnosed with Asperger's Syndrome, a condition she calls her 'superpower'; the ability to see the world in black and white with "no grey areas".

Inspired by the 'March for Our Lives' protests following the school shootings in Florida, USA (2018), Greta organised the 'Fridays for Future' campaign, skipping school on Fridays to stand outside the Swedish parliament with her trusty placard reading 'SKOLSTREJK FÖR KLIMATET' ('School Strike for Climate'). She was (and is) calling for stronger action on climate change, and has since widened her campaign to say this will have a disproportionate effect on young people, and that politicians and those in power should listen to scientists, "unite behind the science and act on the science".

Using social media to spread her message, Greta has definitely had an effect on the world stage. Some notable milestones include:

May 2018 – *Won a climate change essay competition with lines such as "I want to feel safe. How can I feel safe when I know we are in the greatest crisis in human history?"*

24 January 2019 – *Attended the World Economic Forum, Davos, with lines such as "I want you to act as if the house is on fire, because it is".*

May 2019 – *appeared on the cover of Time which called her a 'next generation leader'*

23 September 2019 – *At the UN Climate Action Summit in New York she made a dramatic speech including the famous lines "How dare you!" and "You are failing us!"*

2019 – *UN Climate Change Conference, Madrid.*

Late 2019 – *nominated for Nobel Peace Prize, and won 'Time Person of the Year'*

January 2020 – *At Davos again, saying "You haven't seen anything yet!"*

Despite her passion, not everyone is in agreement with her. For example an article in Spectator (2019) titled 'The Trouble with Greta Thunberg' asks if she is not just "a well-crafted piece of PR"; who would criticize an "untouchable" 16-year-old girl with Asperger's? The article asks if her CO2 emissions targets are realistic, and whether it is right to see things in black and white. Is the world, and specifically climate change, much more complex than that?

Her biggest adversary is none other than Donald Trump, with whom Thunberg has tweeted. The first time was in September 2019 when Trump posted a video of her in which she says "people are dying, whole ecosystems are collapsing. We are in the beginning of a mass extinction" to which Trump wrote the tongue-in-cheek response "She seems like a very happy young girl looking forward to a bright and wonderful future". The second time was after Thunberg won 'Time Person of the Year' which trump thought "so ridiculous" and advised Greta to "work on her anger management problem, then go to a good old-fashioned movie with a friend. Chill Greta, chill!", to which she mocked "(I am) a teenager working on her anger management problem. Currently chilling and watching a good old-fashioned movie with a friend".

And so we come to the World Economic Forum in Davos 2020, happening as I write. At a news conference Greta was upbeat and gave us a taste of things to come: "To the leaders and those in power, I would like to say that you haven't seen anything yet! You haven't seen the last of us. We assure you of that!"

Play: When Thunberg Met Trump

Characters

Host
Greta Thunberg
Donald Trump

Setting

Standing at podiums in Davos, Switzerland

Script

(audience claps)
Host: Hello, and welcome to Davos, Switzerland. We have two guests tonight, Greta Thunberg and Donald Trump. Let's welcome our first guest, Greta Thunberg.
(audience claps)
Greta: Good evening.
Host: Good evening, Greta. How would you describe yourself?
Greta: I am absolutely independent, and do what I do completely for free. I want to feel safe.
Host: And what do you do in your free time?
Greta: I like to chill, and watch old-fashioned movies with friends.
Host: Oh, I see, you only talk in quotes – your own quotes?
Greta: Yes. We must unite behind the science and act on the science.
Host: You are very young. Shouldn't you be at school?
Greta: Yes, this is all wrong. I shouldn't be here. I should be back in school on the other side of the world.
Host: What does a young kid like you know about the world?
Greta: What? How dare you! We are not stupid, yet you all come to us

young people for hope?
Host: Alright, alright! Chill Greta, chill!
Greta: How dare you!
Host: OK. Time to introduce our next guest. Please welcome President Donald Trump.
(audience claps)
Donald: Good evening. Who is this?
Host: This is Greta Thunberg, the climate change activist.
Donald: So ridiculous!
Greta: Hey Trump, change is coming, whether you like it or not.
Donald: What?
Greta: I mean, I want you to act as if the house is on fire, because it is.
Donald: Chill, Greta. You need to work on your anger management problem.
Greta: You are the one with the problem – the eyes of all future generations are upon you. And if you choose to fail us, I say – we will never forgive you.
Donald: Well, I'm gonna get my mop and bucket ready! I'm gonna build a golf course!
Greta: How dare you! You have stolen my dreams and my childhood with your empty words...
Donald: Yawn!
Greta: All you can talk about is money and fairytales of eternal economic growth. How dare you! You are failing us!
Host: Stop! We have to end there – the studio IS on fire!
Donald: Let's get out quick!
Greta: Run!
(they all run off stage)

(All actors take a bow)

Director's Corner

The setting is the World Economic Forum in Davos, Switzerland, and Greta Thunberg prepares to square off with US President Donald Trump. The main thing is to get the reactions between the two, especially rage, anger, disgust and contempt! Thunberg almost seems to spit fire as she speaks, whereas Trump has a laid back confident style. But suddenly they are united in escape from fire!

The Set
- ✓ *three podiums (Greta, Trump and the Host);*
- ✓ *a sign in the background reading 'DAVOS'.*

Costumes and Props Box
- ✓ *Greta wears casual sports clothes and has very long pigtails;*
- ✓ *Trump wears a suit and tie, with a floppy yellow wig.*

Sound and lighting
- ✓ *fire can be represented by coloured paper, in the shape of flames, or by colourful lighting.*

Other considerations
- ✓ *the aim of this play is to contrast two opposing views to climate change;*
- ✓ *see if you can get the real people to attend your school, but don't use real fire.*

Sky Brown: Sky High

In Brief

Aged just 11, Sky Brown will be Great Britain's youngest summer Olympian at Tokyo 2020. The ambitious pre-teen is skateboarding her way in to sports history, as the sport itself also makes its debut at the games.

As a toddler a skateboard was the only toy she never got bored with. She started skating in earnest at age 4, and at first mostly learned her moves from watching YouTube as she searched for new tricks to study and try out.

She became noticed when she was the youngest girl to compete at the Vans US Open Pro Series in 2016, at just 8 years old. She was able to dazzle the audience and the commentator, who said "she skates bigger than she is".

Since then she has had a number of notable successes, including:

Dew Tour Competition, USA (2019) – *came 12th;*
ISO International Championship, China (2019) – *came 5th;*
Park World Skateboarding Championships, Sao Paulo (2019) – *came 3rd;*
Rio (2019) – *came 3rd;*
UK State Nationals (2019) – *came 1st;*
Dancing With The Stars: Juniors (2018) – *came 1st (with JT Church);*
2019 – *nominated for BBC Young Sports Personality of the Year.*

She is now ranked 3rd in the world for women, and 1st in Britain, and all eyes are now firmly set on the 2020 Tokyo Olympics. True to style she is trying to perfect anew move for the Olympics – a 'backside 540' which involves spinning one-and-a-half-times towards your toes (personally I can't even imagine that!). She says she has a lot of tricks to work on; "I can do a Frontside 540 but I'm trying to learn the Backside 540", she says. Of the Olympics she says "It's going to be really cool… you can show what skateboarding is and how creative you can be".

Britain's youngest summer Olympian to date is Margery Hinton at 13 years 43 days in Amsterdam in 1928. But Britain's youngest ever Olympian was at the Lake Placid Winter Olympics (USA, 1980): Cecilia Colledge at 11 years 73 days. When Sky gets to Tokyo she will be 12 years and 12 days old.

What does she want to be when she grows up? "I have a lot of things I want to be" she says: a skateboarder, a surfer, a dancer… for the time being she is pushing boundaries to inspire a new generation: "When I skate I just feel free, like I can do anything. And if people see me, the smallest girl, doing the highest trick, then anyone can think they could do anything".

Play: I Like to Skate High

Characters

Sky Brown
Skater Boy 1 (Jack)
Skater Boy 2 (Josh)
Skater Boy 3 (John)
Judge
Audience

Setting

An urban skate Park in Central London surrounded by apartment blocks and an underground line.

Script

Judge: Welcome to the 2020 London Skateboard Competition! Let's meet our four contestants. The first is Jack, who is 12 and from Chelmsford.
Jack: Hi.
Judge: The second is Josh, who is 13 and from Manchester.
Josh: Hi.
Judge: The third is John, who is 12 and from Uxbridge.
John: Hi.
Judge: And last but not least is Sky, who is 11 and from London.
Sky: Hi. I like to skate high. I like to do spins and kickflips. I like to push boundaries for girls!
(the boys laugh at this)
Judge: OK, it's time to show your best trick. Jack, you're first. What trick

will you perform today?
Jack: I'm gonna do the triple kick double thrust back drop!
Judge: Wow! Let's see it.
(Jack performs the trick, the audience claps)
Judge: Josh, you're next. What trick will you perform today?
Josh: I'm gonna do the back whip drop stab jump!
Judge: Sounds great! Let's see it.
(Josh performs the trick, the audience claps)
Judge: John, you're next. What trick will you perform today?
John: I'm gonna do the up down left right jump stop kick!
Judge: Amazing! Let's see it.
(John performs the trick, the audience claps)

Judge: Sky, you're next. What trick will you perform today?
Sky: I'm gonna do the Backside 540.
Judge: Really? A girl? A little tiny girl?
(the boys laugh at this)
Sky: I like to do tricks that boys are doing because I feel like some boys
think girls can't do what boys can do.
Judge: OK. Let's see it.
(Sky performs the trick, the audience claps and cheers)
Jack: That's amazing!
Josh: Well done!
John: Your ability is endless!
Judge: Yes, Sky, that was excellent. You are the winner!
Sky: Thank you. If people see me, the smallest girl doing the highest
trick, then anyone can think they can do anything!
(the audience claps and cheers)

(All actors take a bow)

Director's Corner

The boys don't believe at first that a "little girl" can perform complicated tricks – but they soon change their minds! There's an element of acrobatics in this play, but I'd recommend fake jumps and turns. Skateboarders have a unique fashion style – make full use of the humorous side of this.

The Set
  ✓ *the skate park can be very simple, similar to a playground with basketball hoops and a goalpost to the side*

Costumes and Props Box
  ✓ *teen 'skateboarder' style – T-shirts, baggy jeans, baseball cap, plimsoles*
  ✓ *some kind of ramp or slope on which to perform 'tricks'*

Sound and Lighting
  ✓ *a tape of background 'playground' noise*

Other Considerations
  ✓ *students can mime the acrobatics rather than actually do it*
  ✓ *how would you decorate your skateboard?*

Coco Gauff: Cocomania

In Brief

It's hard to believe that Cori 'Coco' Gauff is just 15 years old as she strides confidently onto the tennis court with true teen spirit and proceeds to 'demolish' her opponent.

Born on 13th March 2004, Coco was born and raised in Delray Beach, Florida. She became interested in tennis after watching Serena Williams win the 2009 Australian Open on TV, and began playing in earnest at the age of 6. Her first competition success was the 'Little Mo' contest at age 8 (2012). By age 10 (2014) she had joined a tennis academy in France where she first showed 'determination, athleticism and a fighting spirit'. Even at this early time her talent shone through; her coach said "when she looks at you and tells you she will be number one, you can only believe it".

In the early days she competed in the 2017 Junior US Open and finished runner-up — the youngest finalist in the tournament's history; in 2018 she became number 1 junior in the world after the French Open; and in the 2018 US Open she won the doubles alongside Caty McNally.

More recently she started her professional career at Wimbledon in 2019. In her main draw debut she defeated Venus Williams (world number 44) in straight sets. She also defeated world number 60 Polona Hercog. She was only eliminated after losing to Simona Halep, the eventual winner. All four of her matches at Wimbledon were the highest watched matches on US TV, and the event raised her to world number 141.

As I write Coco has just taken part in the Australian Open 2020. She defeated Venus Williams in the first round, Sorana Cirstea in the second, and defending champion Naomi Osaka in the third. She lost in the fourth round to Sofia Kenin.

It was her match against Osaka that drew most headlines. British newspaper The Telegraph described Coco's strokes as "stronger and more accurate" than Osaka's. Indeed, "her serve was more ferocious and her movement twice as proactive". Coco Gauff and Naiomi Osaka have a great camaraderie and friendship; they are simultaneously colleagues and rivals, but share deep respect: the true definition of champions.

Gauff is charitable as well as an inspirational champion. In August 2019 she visited schoolchildren at Village Academy, Palm Beach, on their first day of school. She welcomed and high-fived the kids, gave out special backpacks, and gave a motivational speech. Her message was "Work hard. Dream hard. Anything is possible". As the Telegraph article concludes, when Coco is around, "a peculiar vortex is created... a kind of hysteria". Yes, it's called Cocomania!

Play: The Australian Open: Coco and Naomi

Characters

Coco Gauff
Naomi Osaka
Umpire

Setting

A tennis court at the Australian Open.

Script

Umpire: Last set. In play!

Naomi: Weren't you really young when you started to play tennis?
Coco: Yes, that's right. My first contest was the 'Little Mo' when I was eight.
Naomi: Wow! And what about the 2018 US Open?
Coco: Well, I won the doubles alongside my buddy Caty McNally.
Naomi: And I heard you were at Wimbledon?
Coco: Yeah, I did great. I beat Venus Williams! It was a fantastic time.

Umpire: In! love – 15!

Naomi: How about your training in France? What was it like?

Coco: Oh, that was great, I mean, it was great to be able to train in France. It's a beautiful country and the food is unbelievable.

Umpire: Out! Love all!

Naomi: So when did you get interested in tennis?
Coco: That's easy! I first got interested after I watched Serena Williams play on TV. I mean, it was amazing!
Naomi: It sure was. Oh…

Umpire: Out! 15 -30!

Coco: So what are your plans for the future?
Naomi: My future plan is to beat you in this game!
Coco: Oh no! I can't hit the ball! Looks like your dreams came true!

Umpire: Game, set and match Gauff! Game over!

(All actors take a bow)

Director's Corner

Try to make the interaction between Coco and Naomi to reflect a tennis match – after all, speech is a bit like the back and forth of tennis! The set can be very simple: the outline of a tennis court. At Wimbledon the court is green grass, while at the Australian Open it is an artificial dark blue.

The Set
- ✓ *the lines of a tennis court – use masking tape*
- ✓ *a tennis net*
- ✓ *a chair for the umpire*

Costumes and Props Box
- ✓ *two tennis rackets and a ball*
- ✓ *sports clothes*

Sound and Lighting
- ✓ *the sound of a crowd cheering*

Other Considerations
- ✓ *the theme is camaraderie and friendship in competition*
- ✓ *you might use an invisible ball*

Billie Eilish and Justin Bieber: Bad Guys

In Brief

She never smiles because she says it makes her feel weak and powerless, she doesn't understand peer pressure, and she sings in a whispery and husky voice. Welcome to the world of Billie Eilish!

Born in Los Angeles on 18th December 2001, she grew up in the Highland Park neighbourhood accompanied by 'a lot of gunshots'. Her parents wanted her and her brother, Finneas, to express themselves and explore whatever they wanted. For Finneas this led to performing in a band and writing songs, while for Billie it meant experimenting with acting and singing.

But Billie became famous by accident: she was asked by her teacher to come up with a song that the teacher could choreograph a dance to. It was Billie's brother, Finneas, who offered the song 'Ocean Eyes' which he had originally written for his band. When they placed it on SoundCloud, back in early 2016, it gained 1,000 listens overnight!

One thing led to another, and the song was released by Darkroom and Interscope Records later in 2016. This was quickly followed by a second single, 'Bellyache' in February 2017. She's now become noted for her 'whispery, husky voice' that echoes 'teen-goth angst', not to mention her unusual dress sense, wearing baggy, ill-fitting clothing that, in her words, "looks memorable".

Her personal and musical style is reflected in her song titles: 'When the Party's Over', 'Bury a Friend', and the album 'When We All Fall Asleep, Where Do We Go?'. The album reached number one in both the US and the UK in 2019. So, her bleakness and melancholy style certainly has its followers.

One of her songs, 'Bad Guy', reached number one in the US in July 2019, and featured none other than Justin Bieber. Now 26 years old, Bieber became famous when he was much younger.

Born on March 1st 1994 in Stratford, Ontario, Canada, Bieber's discovery was also by accident. In early 2007, aged 12, he sang Ne-Yo's 'So Sick' in a local talent contest, and came second. It was when his mother posted clips on YouTube that Bieber was spotted by Scooter Braun, a music marketing executive. Later on in 2007 (at age 13) he went to audition in Atlanta where he signed up to Island Records with Braun as his manager.

His first album, 'My World' (2009) was full of the 'teen pop' of his early years, as were early hits like 'Baby' (2010)and 'Boyfriend' (2012). He soon developed a more mature 'dance-pop' style evidenced in his number one album 'Believe' (2012) and number one single 'What Do You Mean?' (2015).

He's experienced both highs and lows. In terms of lows, in March 2013 he fainted backstage at London's O2 Arena after complaining of breathing problems. He was taken to hospital as a precaution but discharged soon after. In February 2019 it was reported that he was being treated for depression, and a month later said that he'd been "feeling super disconnected and weird" and "struggling a lot". In January 2020 he announced he had Lyme Disease, explaining why 'he looked like he was on drugs'.

As for highs, in 2019 he had reportedly sold over 150 million records and had a net worth of$285 million. In his personal life, he married Hailey Baldwin on September 13th 2018 in New York with the words "I can't wait to marry you, baby".

Play: Justin Bieber and Billie Eilish: Bad Guys

Characters

Billie Eilish
Justin Bieber

Setting

A recording studio in Hollywood

Script

Justin: Hey, Billie, is it true that you never smile?
Billie: It's true. I've even got a song called 'Don't Smile At Me'. Smiling makes me feel weak and powerless. Hey, Justin, I hear you're a bad guy!
Justin: Yeah, I'm so criminal, with a bloody nose!
Billie: Woah! So cynical! You're a tough guy!
Justin: Haha! So, tell me about your first single, 'Ocean Eyes'. It became a hit by accident?
Billie: Yeah, my teacher wanted a dance song my brother wrote 'Ocean Eyes'. We put it on SoundCloud and it became a hit! But didn't you become a star by accident, too?
Justin: Yeah, that's right. My mum posted videos of me on YouTube and they were seen by a record producer. Hey, Billie, tell me a bout your

new album.

Billie: Yeah, well, it's called 'When We Fall Asleep, Where Do We Go?'. It's great. How about your music?

Justin: Hmmm, well it used to be teen pop, but now it's more mature. Take a listen to my hit 'What Do You Mean?'. *(he sings a little bit)*

Billie: Who, just can't get enough! I've got Tourettes Syndrome. It means I have a nervous tic and I get depressed. But tell me about your health problems.

Justin: Yeah, I get depressed too, in fact I struggle a lot. And I've got Lyme Disease, so it looks like I'm on drugs! But don't worry cos' I'm a tough guy, I'm a rough guy...

Billie: I like it when you take control. It's my brother, Finneas, who gives me confidence. He writes and produces songs for me. You've got brothers and sisters, haven't you?

Justin: Yeah, there's Jazmyn, my half-sister and Jaxon, my half-brother. And my step-mother's just had a new baby!

Billie: She sounds like an animal!

Justin: I'll be your animal!

Billie: Wow, Justin, I'm wearing your cologne.

Justin: Yeah, I'm the bad guy, duh, I'm the bad guy, duh!

Together: Bad guy, bad guy, baby baby baby, bad guy...

(All actors take a bow)

Director's Corner

These are two iconic stars of modern music, each with a very distinctive style. But they share health problems and a mistrust of authority. The play is a mix of speech and lyrics from the song 'Bad Guy' which the two recorded together.

The Set
   ✓ *microphones, musical instruments, a mixing desk*

Costumes and Props Box
   ✓ *two high stools*
   ✓ *one microphone on a stand in the middle*
   ✓ *Bieber wears hip-hop style – colourful*
   ✓ *Eilish wears baggy clothes – all black*

Sound and Lighting
   ✓ *an excerpt from 'Bad Guy'*

Other Considerations
   ✓ *don't use the whole song, for legal reasons*
   ✓ *are teenagers really lazy, apathetic and naïve?*

The Life and Death of Julius Caesar

In Brief

Julius Caesar is considered by many to be the greatest military commander and dictator in history, and is credited with creating the Roman Empire. However, his youth, ambition and power led to his bloody demise.

Caesar was born into the prestigious Julian family in Subura, Rome, on 13th July 100BC. He was taught by a private tutor from around the age of six, with subjects including reading, writing, Roman law, and public speaking: all of which would prove very important in later life. Though the Julian family were not very influential, they did have some contacts that allowed Caesar to progress within the Roman political system.

The first turning point in Caesar's life was when his father, Cinna, died suddenly and he became the head of the family at the young age of sixteen. He became responsible for his mother, Aurelia, and his sister, Julia. At seventeen he was married to Cornelia, the daughter of a powerful politician in Rome (also called Cinna).

Unfortunately for Caesar this turn of events coincided with a bloody civil war between his uncle, Marius (allied with his father-in-law) and their rival Sulla. Their rival was victorious and Caesar's connections with the failed regime made him a target of aggression: he was stripped of his inheritance and his priesthood, but refused to divorce his wife, Cornelia. It was decided that the best thing would be for Caesar to leave Rome and join the Roman army.

He fought in Spain, France and Asia, and soon gained a good reputation as a military hero and excellent public speaker. He was able to move quickly up the ranks. After the family rival, Sulla, died in 78BC, Caesar was able to return to Rome, this time as a war hero. Again he quickly rose up the ranks, this time of politics and government. Over the years he gained more respect and power until in 44BC he was appointed 'dictator for life' (latin 'dictator perpetuo').

When in power he enacted many reforms, including:

- ❖ He introduced the Julian Calendar, with 365 days and a leap year every four years;
- ❖ He gave citizenship to residents in outlying parts of the Roman republic;
- ❖ He initiated land reform;
- ❖ He controlled and centralised bureaucracy in Rome;
- ❖ He relieved debt for many citizens;
- ❖ He enlarged the Senate (parliament)

Though Caesar was popular, there were some rumbles of discontent. First, the triumphal games, gladiator contests and beast-hunts (with 400 lions) that he ordered were seen as an extravagant waste by many. Second, his populist and authoritarian reforms angered the noble elite, and his success, power and ambition alienated many senators who conspired against him. Finally, many senators held the strong view that Rome should remain a republic rather than an empire as Caesar wanted.

Mark Antony, Caesar's good friend had warned that this would all lead to bad news, with the words "Beware the Ides of March"(the 15th of March, as Shakespeare dramatized it). But this was to no avail. A group of senators, led by Brutus and Cassius, plotted to murder Caesar, and on March 15th 44BC a group of senators led by Brutus and Cassius approached him as he arrived at the Senate building. He tried to wave them away but one of them suddenly grabbed his shoulders and pulled him to the ground and he was stabbed in the neck. Caesar cried "Why, this is violence!" upon which the other senators also produced daggers and began to stab him. Though Caesar attempted to get away, hiding his face with his toga, he tripped and fell. And so his fate was sealed.

Caesar's last words were spoken to Brutus: "You too, child?" or, as Shakespeare dramatized it, "You too, Brutus? Then fall, Caesar". Brutus and the other senators fled the building and marched into Rome shouting "People of Rome, we are once again free!".

The irony is that Caesar was Emperor of Rome for only a year before he was assassinated.

Caesar still retains a strong presence in the modern world, most notably his Julian Calendar which is almost identical to the modern Western calendar. If you go to Rome you can visit Caesar's resting place at the Temple of Caesar, Rome. There are Roman remains throughout mainland Europe, and closer to home we can see a marble bust of Julius Caesar at the British Museum. In 43AD the Romans finally captured and ruled Britain, and Roman remains exist throughout the country such as Hadrian's Wall, Fishbourne Roman Villa, or the segments of wall in the City of London near the Barbican and Museum of London.

Play: The Assassination of Julius Caesar

Characters

Julius Caesar
Teacher
Caesar's Father
Caesar's Mother
Caesar's Sister
Cornelia (Caesar's wife)
Soldiers from Spain, France and Asia (non-speaking)
Roman People
Brutus
Cassius

Setting

A Roman villa with decorated walls and mosaics on the floor.

Script

Scene 1: At School

Caesar: Good morning, teacher.
Teacher: Good morning, boy.
Caesar: What will we study today, teacher?
Teacher: We will study reading and writing.
Caesar: Anything else?

Teacher: We will study Roman politics.
Caesar: Anything else?
Teacher: We will study speaking in public.
Caesar: Great! Thank you, teacher.

Scene 2: Death of Caesar's father

Caesar: Father, what is wrong?
Father: Oh! I am old. I am weak. I am going to die!
Caesar: Oh, father!
Father: Goodbye! *(he dies)*
Caesar: Father is dead. Now I must look after my mother and sister.
Mother: Don't worry, Julius.
Sister: We will help you.
Cornelia: I will help you, too. Let's get married!
Caesar: Great idea!
(everyone claps and cheers)

Scene 3: In the Roman Army

Cornelia: You can't stay in Rome, it's too dangerous.
Caesar: what shall I do?
Cornelia: You must join the Roman army.
Caesar: Good idea! Goodbye!
(he fights soldiers from France, Spain and Asia, and kills them)
Cornelia: Well done!
Caesar: Yeah! My enemies are dead! I will return to Rome.

Scene 4: Becoming Emperor

People: Caesar is good! Caesar is great! Caesar will help us!
Caesar: Hello, my people. I am good. I will help you.

People: How will you help us?
Caesar: I will give you money.
People: Anything else?
Caesar: I will give you land.
People: Anything else?
Caesar: I will give you a new government.
People: Anything else?
Caesar: I will give you a new calendar.
People: Hooray!
(the people clap and cheer)

Scene 5: Assassination

Brutus: I don't like Caesar.
Cassius: I don't like Caesar either.
Brutus: He is too powerful.
Cassius: He is too ambitious.
Brutus: He is too wasteful.
Cassius: We must kill him.
(they go to the senate, and Caesar enters)
Brutus: Caesar!
Caesar: Yes?
Brutus: *(he holds a dagger)* Take this!
Cassius: And this! *(he stabs Caesar)*
Caesar: Why, this is violence! You too, Brutus? Then fall, Caesar!
(he falls and dies)
Brutus and Cassius: People of Rome, we are free!

(All actors take a bow)

Director's Corner

The assassination of Julius Caesar is one of the most dramatic moments in history, cementing Caesar's image as the greatest Emperor. Here the script builds to that dramatic moment which can be great fun to act: think plastic daggers and ketchup.

The Set
✓ *walls decorated with murals of Roman warriors and wild animals;*
✓ *colourful mosaic on the floor (an art project in itself)*

Costumes and Props Box
✓ *Caesar's toga (robe) and head wreath;*
✓ *Roman costumes – a toga can be made from a white sheet*
✓ *plastic or foam daggers*
✓ *ketchup (be careful!)*

Lighting and Sound
✓ *minimal lighting is needed;*
✓ *sounds of fighting and battle*

Other Considerations
✓ *don't use real daggers;*
✓ *the moral is that sometimes even your best and trusted friends can turn on you.*

Tutankhamun: The Boy King

In Brief

Tutankhamun is the world's most famous pharaoh. His tomb was discovered by Howard carter in 1922 and to his astonishment the tomb was packed with precious and invaluable artefacts. Carter's discovery has stirred up a lot of interest in Tutankhamun and ancient Egypt in general.

Tutankhamun ruled Egypt as pharaoh for ten years until his death aged just nineteen. Because of this he is known as 'The Boy King'. He was not considered to be very important in ancient times, and was not recorded on most lists of ancient kings. He only came to power after his father, Akhenaten, was forced to abdicate following an increasingly autocratic and corrupt regime. Even during his reign he achieved little and relied heavily on his powerful advisors Ay and Horemheb.

But he did manage some achievements. Under the guidance of Ay and Horemheb he had the Royal Court moved back to Thebes, and reversed the religious reform of his father. He sought to restore the old order, hoping that the gods would once again look favourably on Egypt. He initiated a vast building project at Karnak where he dedicated a temple to Amun, the creator sun-god. He also ordered the repair of holy sites, and the completion of the red granite lions at Soleb.

It is the manner of his death that has been the subject of much research, but the general conclusion is that it was sudden and unexpected. Tutankhamun had suffered from adverse medical conditions for some time. He was tall and physically frail, and had bone disease in his left foot. CT scans in 1995 showed an infection in his left leg, whist DNA from his mummy showed evidence of multiple malaria infections. DNA pointed to mosquito-bourn parasites that cause malaria. This would have weakened his immune system and slowed down the healing process.

Further X-rays have shown he suffered from Klippel-Feil Syndrome – the fusion of two or more of the spine bones. Apparently all seven of these in his neck were fused together, meaning he was unable to move his head from side to side. Added to this was that he required the use of a cane to walk; and all this ultimately led to his early death.

The discovery of Tutankhamun's tomb was the one moment that led to his infamy. Howard Carter was employed by George Herbert, Earl of Carnarvon, to start an intense search for the tomb in the Valley of the Kings. They eventually did find the tomb in the Valley of the Kings. The day and time were chosen to unseal the tomb, with around twenty appointed witnesses including Egyptian officials and museum staff. So, on November 26th 1922 Carter and Herbert became the first people to enter the tomb in over 3,000 years.

Shortly after the burial chamber was opened, and showed the first glimpse of the sarcophagus of Tutankhamun. This interior chamber contained another great surprise: it was full of precious and priceless artefacts! 5,398 objects were found in all, including a solid gold coffin, thrones, archery bows, trumpets, food and wine, oils and perfumes, and a dagger with an iron blade made from a meteorite. The gem was the elaborate golden burial mask of Tutankhamun, made of solid gold and decorated with precious stones. It took Carter and his team ten years to empty and catalogue the contents of the tomb.

A 'curse of the pharaohs' exists, with early death proclaimed for those who enter the tomb. This was proven with the death of the Earl of Carnarvon himself on 5th April 1923; though others present at the tomb's opening went on to enjoy long and healthy lives – a study showed that of the fifty-eight people present at the tomb's opening, only eight died within a dozen years.

Tutankhamun has not just stayed in Egypt – he's gone on a world tour! The best known exhibition tour was 'The Treasures of Tutankhamun' which ran from 1972 to 1979 and was first shown at the British Museum in London. To this day it remains the most popular exhibition in the museum's history with 1.7 million people attending. The Metropolitan Museum of Art in New York organised the US leg of the tour (1976-9) when 8 million people attended.

The latest exhibition is the 'Tutankhamun: Treasures of the Golden Pharaoh' exhibition held at the Saatchi Gallery in London. It is billed as the largest collection of ancient Egyptian treasures to come to London since 'The Treasures of Tutankhamun'. There are over 150 artefacts, but not the iconic gold face mask. You can visit for an eye-watering £28.50.

Unless you're in time to catch the latest exhibition in London, your best bet is to go to Egypt itself. Wait for the brand new 'Grand Egyptian Museum' to open in 2021, or content yourself with the Giza pyramids and sphynx. One thing is for sure: the discovery of his tomb in 1922 has made him Tutankhamun the most well-known pharaoh of modern times.

Play: A Visit to Tutankhamun

Characters

Tutankhamun
Howard Carter
Earl of Carnarvon

Setting

King Tutankhamun's ante-chamber filled with golden artefacts, precious jewels and mummies

Script

(Carter and Carnarvon are moving a stone from the entrance to Tutankhamun's tomb)
Carter: Just move this big stone to the side.
Carnarvon: It's very heavy.
Carter: Push, push! Look! There he is!
Tutankhamun: Hello, Mr. Carter. It's been a long time.
Carter: Hello, King Tutankhamun. Yes, it's been a long time. This is my friend, Earl Carnarvon.
Carnarvon: Pleased to meet you. King Tutankhamun.
Tutankhamun: The pleasure is mine. How can I help you this time, Mr. Carter?
Carter: We'd like some information about ancient Egypt, for our news report.
Tutankhamun: OK, I can help you.
Carter: First, how old are you, and when were you born?
Tutankhamun: I am 19 years old. I was born in 1341 BC.

Carnarvon: Your artefacts… tell me about your artefacts…

Tutankhamun: Of course. There are 5,398 artefacts in my tomb, all of them priceless. Look! Here is my archery bow! Here is my golden dagger! Here is my trumpet! Here is my food and wine!

Carter: Next we'd like to know about the monuments and temples you erected.

Tutankhamun: Monuments and temples? Well, at Karnak I dedicated a temple to Amun, the creator sun-god. I completed the red granite lions at Soleb. Also I had the holy sites repaired that my father destroyed.

Carnarvon: And how about the struggle against your father? He abdicated and you took over, right?

Tutankhamun: That's a good question. I didn't like my father. He changed many things. When he died I moved the Royal Court back to Thebes, and reversed the religious reforms he had made.

Carter: Finally, a really important question: how did you die?

Tutankhamun: Yes, yes, I am dead. How did I die? Well, I was always a little bit frail and ill, with weak bones, then an infection in my left leg, then a malarial infection that weakened my immune system, then… the end! Death!

Carter: Thank you King Tutankhamun. You've been really helpful.

Tutankhamun: You're welcome. By the way, I hear the world has forgotten me? Fiddlesticks! You will tell the world how great I am! Take my artefacts on a world tour and open a new museum in Cairo!

Carter: Of course, King Tutankhamun!

Tutankhamun: Excellent. May the sun god look well upon you!

(the stone magically moves back over the entrance)

Carnarvon: He is a good King, isn't he?

Carter: Yes. Next time we will stay for dinner! *(they laugh)*

(All actors take a bow)

Director's Corner

As one of the most dramatic stories in history, the discovery of Tutankhamun's tomb offers great scope for dramatization. Think gold, gold and more gold! Your Tutankhamun actor need not be a boy; a girl could play the part equally well. Tutankhamun should have a regal and confident style.

The Set
- ✓ *Egyptian hieroglyphics hang from the walls*
- ✓ *there is lots of gold everywhere*

Costumes and Props Box
- ✓ *a shovel and pick-axe for the two men*
- ✓ *a fine costume for Tutankhamun*
- ✓ *Tutankhamun holds a golden spear and sits on a golden throne*
- ✓ *gold artefacts: archery bow, dagger, trumpet*
- ✓ *a large 'rock' to roll over the doorway (card or polystyrene)*

Sound and Lighting
- ✓ *a flash of light when we first see Tutankhamun*
- ✓ *the sound of a trumpet*

Other Considerations
- ✓ *The British Museum in London has a large collection of mummies*
- ✓ *don't use real gold – it's too expensive!*

Pocahontas: Powhatan Princess

In Brief

Pocahontas means 'playful one'. She was a Native American who befriended settlers of the colony of Jamestown, Virginia, marrying one of them and travelling to England. She is credited as a symbol of bringing the Native American Indian and Western European peoples together. Her most heroic moment came when she saved the Englishman, John Smith, from execution.

Pocahontas was the daughter of Powhatan, chief of an alliance of around thirty Algonquian tribes. She had a peaceful and happy childhood, much like any other, and performed daily tasks such as looking for firewood, farming, and helping with construction. She was certainly not a 'princess'!

Life went on as normal until April 1607 when over one hundred settlers from Europe arrived, led by colonist John Smith. The relationship between the settlers and the Native Indians was tense, and apart from occasional trade the two sides kept pretty much to themselves.

While exploring the Chickahominy River in December 1607 Smith was captured by a native hunting party and taken to Chief Powhaton's camp at Werowocomoco. During his capture he became familiar with Pocahontas, then only 11 or 12 years old, and taught each other some basic words of their languages. So Pocahontas was dismayed when the chief ordered Smith's execution! What could she do? This man who had shown her kindness must be saved!

Smith was due to be executed by a blow to the head with a rock club. However, at the moment of execution, Pocahontas begged her father for mercy, which he duly gave, so saving Smith from execution. John Smith was allowed to return to Jamestown.

After this event relations between the colonists and Native Indians improved greatly; Pocahontas befriended Smith and often visiting the colony in Jamestown, sometimes bringing them food as gifts from her father. By 1609 the two sides traded a lot, but that was to change when Smith was injured in a gunpowder accident and had to return to England. In his absence relations again deteriorated. Pocahontas did not return to the colony for some time.

The tense situation reached a head in 1613 when Sir Samuel Argall managed to take Pocahontas prisoner and took her on board his ship. Argall's idea was to use her as a hostage to demand the return of several of his men. With this in mind, Pocahontas was taken to Jamestown. During her 'captivity' (if you can call it that) she was treated well and with courtesy. She was even baptised and converted to Christianity, taking the name 'Rebecca'. After she married John Rolfe in 1614 relative peace and calm ensued. A year after they married she gave birth to a son, Thomas.

In spring 1616 they set sail with a small group to England, docking in Plymouth later that year. The Virginia Company saw this as a chance to publicise the company and win the support of King James I, as well as investors. Pocahontas was presented as a 'princess', and though treated well in London she was seen more as a curiosity than a princess. She wore fancy clothes and went to fashionable parties. She was even brought before King James I.

By 1617 the plan was to return to Virginia, but as luck would have it Pocahontas fell seriously ill and their ship had to dock at Gravesend. Unfortunately she died soon after of pneumonia or tuberculosis. She was buried at St. George's church in March 1617. The church was destroyed by fire in 1727, her grave along with it. Rolfe returned to Virginia; their son, Thomas, stayed in London until 1635 when he too returned to Virginia.

The symbolism of Pocahontas rescuing Smith, then taking on a western lifestyle has endured for centuries in American literature and art. The film 'Pocahontas' (Disney, 1995) portrays the myth that she was head-over-heals in love with Smith, reinforcing a romantic theme of assimilation and the dramatic meeting of two cultures. However, there is no evidence to suggest that she had romantic relations with Smith; rather her true love lay with Rolfe. Though the movie conveyed more myth than truth, it nonetheless made the Native American the star, the main character. And her story helps to understand Native Americans and their history, especially what they went through at the time of European conquest.

Play: Pocahontas in Love

Characters

Pocahontas
Chief Powhatan
John Smith
John Rolfe
King James
Colonists

Setting

The American outback: scrubby lowlands, patches of green trees

Script

Smith: Welcome to Virginia! Welcome to our new world! Welcome to our new home!
Colonists: Hooray! *(they clap and cheer)*
Smith: We will be happy. We will be healthy. We will be rich!
Colonists: Hooray! *(they clap and cheer)*
Smith: We will build a new town: Jamestown.
Colonists: Hooray! *(they clap and cheer)*

Pocahontas: Oh, darling father!
Chief: Oh, darling Pocahontas!
Pocahontas: I love you!

Chief: I love you! You are my delight and darling.
Pocahontas: Thank you father. What will we do today?
Chief: Let's feed the animals and collect firewood.
(they go out to collect firewood)
Pocahontas: Who are those people?
Chief: I don't know. They are strangers. Let's go home.

Smith: Let's explore.
Rolfe: Yes, let's explore. Where?
Smith: Let's go to the Chickahominy River.
Rolfe: Let's go!
(suddenly Powhatan and some warriors appear)
Chief: Take those men! Take that man!
(they scuffle, Rolfe runs away, Smith is captured)
Smith: Oh, no. Ahhhhhh!
Chief: Take this stranger back to camp.

(Smith is tied to a pole)
Smith: Who are you? What are you doing?
Chief: I am Chief Powhatan. I am strong. I am powerful. You are bad. I will kill you!
(Pocahontas runs in)
Pocahontas: Father, stop! Don't kill this man! He is not bad, he is good. Please, father, please!
Chief: *(he thinks)* Hmmm... OK. He can go back to Jamestown.
Smith: Why did you save me?
Pocahontas: Oh, darling John!
Smith: Oh, darling Pocahontas!
Pocahontas: I love you!
Smith: I love you!

(Pocahontas visits Jamestown)
Pocahontas: Here is some food from my father. Where is John Smith?
Rolfe: I'm sorry, he was injured and had to go back to England.
Pocahontas: Oh, no. What's your name?
Rolfe: My name is John Rolfe. I am a successful tobacco farmer. I will teach you English.
Pocahontas: I will teach you my language.
Rolfe: You are beautiful. Let's get married! Let's go to England together!
Pocahontas: That's a good idea.
(they sail to England)

Rolfe: This is King James.
Pocahontas: Hello. My name is Princess Pocahontas.
King: Good to meet you. Where are you from?
Pocahontas: I am from Virginia in North America.
King: Welcome to England.
Rolfe: Thank you King James.
Pocahontas: Oh, darling John!
Rolfe: Oh, darling Pocahontas!
Pocahontas: I love you!
Rolfe: I love you!

(All actors take a bow)

Director's Corner

The story is a milestone in European / Colonial and Native American relations, and Pocahontas has become a symbol of closer relations between the two. As a princess, Pocahontas can be dressed in fine clothes with brilliant jewellery. The most dramatic moment is when she saves Smith from death, and they fall in love!

The Set
- green hills and a few trees made of cardboard

Costumes and Props Box
- native Indian clothes; a headband of feathers
- colonial clothes – formal
- a post, to which Smith can be tied with rope
- grand clothes for the King

Sound and Lighting
- lighting to represent fire as Smith is tied to the post
- tape of Native Indian chanting

Other Considerations
- choose your most beautiful student for the part of Pocahontas
- it is interesting to do a project on early American settlers.

Dick Whittington and His Cat

In Brief

One of the most well-known characters of British folklore is Dick Whittington. He famously overcame poverty and a third-class lifestyle to become the Lord Mayor of London. But it was not his intention – it was only when he tried to leave London that the church bells called him back with the iconic words "Turn again, Whittington, Lord Mayor of London". Incredibly, he kept his obedient cat, Boots, with him throughout the saga, and it was the cat's ability to catch mice and rats that helped a young Dick to his prestigious post.

Dick Whittington was born in the countryside and for the first years of his life was poor, hungry and knew nothing of the city. He came to hear tales of London where the streets were paved with gold. With gold? His curiosity got the better of him and he set off with his trusty cat, Boots, to find his fortune.

But London was not what he expected: overcrowded, dirty streets, with a lot of people who had no time for him. What's more, the streets were not paved with gold! He eventually found work in a shop, moving boxes and delivering parcels to rich people. The job did not pay well, and his cat was little help in his toils. So Dick decided to leave and go back to his village. He said farewell to the shopkeeper and made his way north, into the rolling hills above London. But then something strange happened: as Dick and Boots walked up the steep slopes of Highgate Hill he heard the bells of Bow Church ring. They appeared to call to him, speaking the words "Turn again Whittington, Lord Mayor of London". Dick and Boots looked at each other. Could church bells really speak? Surely not. But

Dick took this as a sign and returned to the city.

He was amazed to find the place filled with unfriendly rats that ate all the people's food and destroyed their houses. Boots, however, did not see the problem and happily ran around town catching all the rats. The King noticed this and asked whose cat it was. It was Dick's. The King was very pleased, and immediately gave Dick his own horse, lots of gold, and made him Lord Mayor of London. Dick was a very worthy Lord Mayor, building houses, a college and a library for the poor. The King, Dick, Boots and all the city people were very happy.

What evidence of Dick Whittington can we see today? Probably most familiar are the many pantomimes that take up his story, often with a lot of humour. These pantomimes have their roots in the nineteenth century when this style of performance became popular. In London the Whittington Stone stands at the foot of Highgate Hill (close to the modern Wittington Stone pub). Though the stone was erected in 1821, the cat atop it was only added in 1964. In the City of London is St. Michael Patenoster Royal Church where Dick is buried; a plaque and stained glass window commemorate him. On College Hill nearby, there is another, similar plaque. Unfortunately, the exact location of Dick's grave has been lost over the years.

The Whittington Hospital (with its own trusty cat) stands on Highgate Hill, and is reputed to be the spot where Dick 'turned again'. Outside London, Whittington Castle stands in the village of Whittington, Shropshire. It was fully renovated and a tearoom and visitor attraction added in 2007, and was opened that year by the Duke of Gloucester. So don't ever give up – "turn again" just like Dick and Boots, and with perseverance you can achieve what you like!

Play: Turn Again Whittington

Characters

Dick Whittington
Boots (Dick's Cat)
Shop Owner
King
The Church Bells
Rats (unspoken part)

Setting

Medieval London, timber-framed houses and cobbled streets, with green hills in the far distance

Script

Dick: Come on, Boots, let's go and find our fortune in London.
Boots: Meow! London?
Dick: Yes, Boots – London. They say the streets are paved with gold.
Boots: Meow! Gold? Meow!

Dick: *(to shop owner)* We are tired. We are hungry. Do you have a place for us to stay?
Shop Owner: Tired? Hungry? A place to stay? You have to work for your food and bed. Work!
Dick: OK. What shall I do?
Shop Owner: Move these boxes! Sweep the floor! Deliver these heavy boxes to the other side of town! Do it! Now!
Dick: Yes, yes, yes... *(Dick moves the boxes, sweeps the floor, and*

delivers the heavy boxes to the other side of town) Boots, will you help me?

Boots: Meow! I'm a cat. I can't help. Sorry!

Dick: How about rats? Can you catch some rats?

Boots: Meow! No, I'm sleepy. When are we going home?

Dick: Let's go now. London is hard work, and this shop owner pays very little money. *(they walk up into the green hills; they hear something...)*

Church Bells: Dick, Dick, listen. Don't go, don't go. Come back to London, you will be rich, come back to London, you will be famous, turn again Dick Wittington, Lord Mayor of London!

Dick: What? Did the church bells speak to me?

Boots: Meow! Yes, I think they did!

Dick: I will not give up! I will not leave London!

Church Bells: Turn again, Wittington, Lord Mayor of London!

Boots: Meow! Look, a fine house. A fine house with lots of rats. I can help. I can catch all the rats. *(Boots chases and catches all the rats)*

King: Look! All the rats are gone! Whose cat is this?

Dick: It is my cat, Your Majesty. My name is Dick.

King: Your cat is a very good cat. And you are a good boy, Dick. Please, stay here with your cat and keep the rats away!

Boots: Meow! Yes, thank you, King.

King: And you, Dick, will be my Lord Mayor of London.

Dick: Yes, thank you, King. *(the King presents Dick and Boots with fine clothes and horses and lots of gold; they are all happy)*

King: *(speaks to audience)* Maybe next time it will be your turn?!

Everybody: Hooray for the King! Hooray for Boots! Hooray for Dick Wittington, Lord Mayor of London! *(they all clap and cheer).*

(All actors take a bow)

Director's Corner

You can use one set for all the parts, maybe hills on the left, medieval houses on the right. The part of Boots could be played by a (suitably dressed) student, or a toy cat can be used with the spoken words voiced over – it depends how many people are at hand. The King could be sitting on a throne, and he can also give a 'horse' for Boots to ride, which could be quite humorous!

The Set
- ✓ *hills and woods*
- ✓ *medieval (timber-framed) buildings*

Costumes and Props Box
- ✓ *boxes and a broom*
- ✓ *toy rat(s)*
- ✓ *hand-bell(s)*
- ✓ *some gold coins*
- ✓ *King's crown and red robe (think 'curtains')*
- ✓ *Lord Mayor's hat and robe*
- ✓ *horses (large cardboard cut-outs)*

Sound and Lighting
- ✓ *church bells (represented by hand-bells?)*

Other considerations
- ✓ *do not use a real cat ;-)*
- ✓ *the moral is that, with perseverance, you can achieve anything you want*

Harry Potter and Friends

In Brief

You might think that with all the talk of magic and wizardry that Harry Potter is fiction, a part of some author's imagination. But no! Harry Potter is real! Hermione Granger is real too! And so is Ron Weasley! How do I know? Because I met them at Platform 9¾ at Kings Cross station!

Harry told me all about himself while waiting for his train to Scotland. He didn't want to retell his story, or recount the plot of the 500 million books written about him. When I mentioned the Warner Bros films about him he gave me a look that could kill. He said that he is quite a normal teenager, really. But Harry – you're worth $25 million!

So what is Harry Potter's character? What is his personality? And how about his pals Hermione and Ron? I asked him.

"Me?" Harry asked, "well, I'm brave, courageous and selfless. I love sharing things with others, especially people I know well. Oh, and I've got great leadership skills. But I have a negative side, I think: I'm quite moody and can have quite a hot temper. I can be a bit impulsive and irrational, I mean, sometimes I act before I think. But I guess I just follow my instinct, and I'm sure what I'm doing is right. That makes me very confident, I suppose".

So, how about his pals Hermione and Ron? Of Hermione he put forward "She's a great friend, very intelligent and hardworking, and she has a very focused and logical mind, but she can be a bit bookish and close-minded. But her quick-thinking has often helped Ron and myself to get out of sticky situations, I mean, she's great at solving riddles or clues".

OK, I then asked about Ron. He's a bit of a weaky, isn't he? Harry gave me a funny look then explained "That's what people who don't know him think. Actually, he's a very loyal friend, almost like a brother to me. He's very supportive and would even give up his life for me or Hermione. And he makes sound choices based on common sense. So no, he's not a weaky!". Right, that's me told!

It was getting late at Kings Cross and they had to catch their train to Hogwarts. So I asked all of them what their secret is. OK, I got it, none of them are weak, so what are their strengths?

Hermione went first. "Well, I suppose my real strengths are that I am logical and focused". "I agree with that" said Ron, "and I'm NOT weak! My personality is more hidden, and my strengths are loyalty and common sense". "Yes" said Harry, "we are a golden trio. Here's our train. Goodbye".

Yes, this 'golden trio' of Harry, Hermione and Ron work well together as each brings different strengths to the table. Their personalities work in harmony and balance each other out. I agree with their online fans that they are intentionally complementary, and that it is difficult to imagine how any one could survive without the others.

So there you have it, Potter fans. Harry potter is the unintentional hero whose main character traits are bravery and selflessness, Hermione Granger the intellectual with a bookish personality, whilst Ron Weasley is the loyal friend who balances out the other two. And I should know – I actually met them!

Play: Platform 9¾

Characters

Narrator
Harry Potter
Hermione Granger
Ron Weasley

Setting

Platform 9¾ at King's Cross station, London.

Script

Narrator: You'll never guess who I bumped in to at King's Cross station the other day. None other than Harry Potter! What's more, Hermione and Ron were there too! So this is the story which he told me on Platform 9¾.

Scene 1: Platform 9¾

Harry: Hurry up Ron, we're going to miss the train!
Ron: I'm coming, Harry. But where is Hermione?
Harry: Huh, girls! She's gone to get something from the shops.
Ron: How long have we got?
Harry: About ten minutes. Come on, let's load the cases onto the train.
(they load the cases on to the train)

Scene 2: On the train
Hermione: Wow, I made it in time!
Ron: Yes, you nearly missed the train.
Hermione: What's Harry doing?
Ron: Oh, he's gone to the restaurant car. He's hungry.
Hermione: Oh, great idea! I'm hungry too!
Ron: Let's go!

Scene 3: In the restaurant car
Harry: A chicken sandwich and a coke, please.
Assistant: Here you are. That's five pounds, please.
Harry: Five pounds? That's expensive!
Assistant: Take it or leave it.
Harry: Hang on a minute, I recognise you. You are Dr. Countbad, the most horrible and terrible person in the world!
Assistant: Yes! You got it! And I've come to kill you, Harry Potter!
(he ties Harry up with rope and puts him in a box)
Harry: Help! Ron? Hermione? Where are you? Help!

Scene 4: Later, in the restaurant car
Ron: Where's Harry? He should be here.
Hermione: Hmmm, yes, where is he? There must be some clues.
Ron: Look! A small piece of rope. What does it mean?
Hermione: Look! A part of Harry's coat! Let me think... *(she thinks)* I know! Someone has taken Harry and tied him up with rope.
Ron: Oh, no! What can we do?
Hermione: We must try to find him. You look over here. I'll look over there. Meet back here in five minutes.
Ron: OK.

Scene 5: In the guard's compartment

Dr. Countbad: Now I have you, Harry! You are tied up with strong rope and in a box! You can not run away.
Harry: You are very bad, Dr. Countbad. Let me go!
Dr. Countbad: Never! Now, what shall I do with you? Feed you to the dragons? Put you in the squashing machine? Turn you into an insect? Oh, such pleasure!
Harry: You will never get away with it!
Dr. Countbad: Now is your end!
(suddenly)
Ron: That's what you think, Dr. Countbad!
Hermione: Don't worry Harry, we will save you.
Dr. Countbad: Never! Here is an evil magic spell... *(he waves his magic wand and smoke appears)* What? Nothing happened!
Hermione: Ha! That's right! That is not your magic wand. I found the clues in the restaurant car, the piece of rope and Harry's coat, and knew it must be you, Dr. Countbad. So I changed your magic wand when you weren't looking. In your hand you have a stick!
Dr. Countbad: A stick! You horrible children! You will pay for this!
(suddenly he disappears in a puff of smoke)
Harry: Thanks, guys. You can untie the rope now.
Ron: No, I think you look good in your box.
Hermione: And tied up with rope!
(they all laugh)

(All actors take a bow)

Director's Corner

Everyone is familiar with Harry and his pals, and here is your chance to act out a real-life Harry Potter play. Choose a confident student to be Harry, and one of your troublemakers to play Dr. Countbad. All scenes can take place on the same set – a railway carriage on a steam train.

The Set
- ✓ *carriage windows, and chairs arranged in two rows opposite each other*

Costumes and Props Box
- ✓ *school uniforms for the children*
- ✓ *a mask and cape for Dr. Countbad*
- ✓ *magic wand(s)*
- ✓ *rope*
- ✓ *a large box*

Sound and Lighting
- ✓ *a 'flash' for when Dr. Countbad disappears*
- ✓ *background noise of a train going over tracks*

Other Considerations
- ✓ *try to put some personality into Harry, Ron and Hermione's character*
- ✓ *the theme is that good will always overcome evil.*

Huckleberry Finn and Friends

In Brief

There are three main characters in The Adventures of Huckleberry Finn: Finn himself, Jim, a black slave, and Tom Sawyer. Though fictitious characters, they portray life in mid-nineteenth century Missouri, Mississippi, and parade the central theme of 'freedom' in society. What does it mean to be 'free'?

'Huck' is the narrator, the son of the local drunk in St. Petersburg, a town on the Mississippi River. Though uneducated, he is thoughtful and intelligent. He is a shrewd judge of character, and has a good, if naïve, sense of morality. He often seems at odds with the 'civilised' world, whose norms are a good education, attending church regularly, and polite manners. This is especially the case when we remember Huck's father is a violent drunkard who certainly does not conform to society's norms.

Huck takes the chance to escape the confines of life (as he sees it) by sailing his raft down the Mississippi River alongside his good friend, Jim, a slave. Jim himself, a grown and mild-mannered man of large build, has a practical and mature approach to life, and is able to show great acts of selflessness. Though a household slave, he is able to form a great bond with Huck which certainly helps them on their journey down the river. But his status also means he is at the mercy of almost all the other characters in the novel.

The other character of note is Tom Sawyer, previously introduced in the previous book 'The Adventures of Tom Sawyer'. Tom is Huck's best friend and peer, and in literary terms serves as a foil to Huck. Tom is imaginative, dominating, and given to wild plans taken from the stories of adventure novels. But he adheres to society's norms and values in a way that Huck struggles with. Tom is noted in the book as "the best fighter and the smartest kid in town".

When Huck and Jim come across each other they hatch a plan to go to the state of Illinois where Jim can live as a free man. On this journey they come across many adventures and wonderful characters: slave traders, con men, and ultimately, by chance, they come across Tom Sawyer's aunt and uncle, Silas and Sally Phelps. They mistake Huck for Tom, who himself turns up to reveal that Jim has been a free man all along according to a provision in his late owner's will.

The Adventures of Huckleberry Finn is acclaimed as a colourful depiction of life, people and places along the Mississippi in the mid nineteenth century. It has central themes of race and identity, especially in the case of Jim who is good-hearted and moral (in contrast to many of the white characters); Huck himself is at odds with the normal values of society, especially his friendship with Jim. Society itself is at fault: Twain has 'Pap' enslave, isolate and beat his son. With a father like this, no wonder Huck has problems fitting into society!

Play: The Adventures of Jim, a Slave

Characters

Jim (narrator)
Miss Watson
Huckleberry Finn
Tom Sawyer
Sally Phelps

Setting

The banks of the Mississippi River, wooden log houses

Script

Jim: Hello, my name's Jim and I'm a slave. Or at least I *was* a slave until a couple of months ago. Do you want to know my story?

Scene 1: Miss Watson's House

Miss Watson: Can you wash all the pots now, Jim? And when you've finished you can scrub the floor and clean the windows.
Jim: Very good, Miss, I'll do that. *(he starts to work)*
Huck: Hey, Jim, you work really hard. Why do you work so hard?
Jim: Well, hello, Master Huck, you see, I work really hard because I'm a slave.
Huck: A slave? What's that?

Jim: It means I have to work for Miss Watson. I wash the pots, scrub the floor, and clean the windows.

Husk: Are you happy?

Jim: I guess so. I have good food and a warm place to sleep. But sometimes I dream...

Husk: What do you dream of, Jim?

Jim: Sometimes I dream that I am free!

Miss Watson: Ha! Jim! You will be free over my dead body!

Jim: I'm sure that is true, Miss Watson.

Scene 2: By the River

Tom: Hi, Huck.

Huck: Hi, Tom.

Tom: What are you up to today?

Huck: Well, I was talking to Jim at Miss Watson's house.

Tom: Jim? The slave?

Huck: Yes, that's right. He dreams of being a free man, but he is a slave. He can't travel. He can't go to the big city. He has to work for Miss Watson.

Tom: He wants to be a free man? We can help him. I can make a plan. *(he thinks)* OK, this is what we're gonna do... *(he whispers in Huck's ear)*

Scene 3: Miss Watson's House

Huck: Jim! Jim! Over here!

Jim: Who said that? What? Eh?

Tom: Over here!

Jim: Oh, it's you, Master Huck and Master Tom. How can I help you?

Huck: We're gonna help *you*, Jim.

Tom: Yes, we're gonna help you to escape!

Jim: Escape? You mean run away? But how?
Huck: Follow us.
Tom: We have a raft to sail down the river.
Huck: You can be a free man!
Jim: OK, let's go!

Scene 4: On the River / Aunt sally's House

(they sit on the raft and sail down the river)
Huck: Where shall we go?
Tom: Let's go to see my Aunt Sally, she lives downriver.
Huck: And what about Jim?
Tom: He can hide in the trees, and we can bring him food.
Jim: See you later. *(he goes to hide in the trees)*
Aunt Sally: Oh, Tom, welcome! And who's your friend?
Tom: This is Huck.
Aunt Sally: Hello, Huck. Won't you boys come in for tea? Kettle's on!
Tom: Thank you, Aunt Sally.
(they follow Aunt Sally into the house)
Aunt Sally: Did you hear about old Miss Watson?
Huck: You mean Jim's owner?
Aunt Sally: Yes, that's right. She died yesterday, unfortunately.
Tom: Oh, poor Jim. He loved Miss Watson. He must be very sad.
Aunt Sally: Oh, but we can't find Jim. He must be very upset. Do you know where he is?
Huck: Yes, we do. He's with us. He's just outside in the trees.
Aunt sally: In the trees? Why is he in the trees?
Tom: Because he's a slave. He wants to be free.
Aunt Sally: But he *is* free! You see, Miss Watson's will says that when she dies, Jim is free.

(suddenly Jim walks in)
Jim: is it true? Am I free? Am I free?
Aunt Sally: Yes, Jim, you are free.
Jim: *(he jumps for joy)* I'm free! I'm free! I'm free!
Huck: Jim is free!
Tom: Jim is free!
Aunt sally: Jim is free!
(they all jump for joy and sing a little song)
Everyone: *(they sing)* We're free, we're free, freedom! Freedom!

(All actors take a bow)

Director's Corner

Freedom is a central theme of the book, as is the contrast between polite and ill-mannered society. There are two locations for this play: by and on the river, and inside a house (Miss Watson's house and Aunt Sally's house can be the same set). There are lots more characters in the original story and you can add them if you want (Huck's drunken father, or the conmen, for example).

The Set
- ✓ *the kitchen of a farmhouse – a dining table and chairs, kitchen equipment, an old stove*
- ✓ *the banks of the Mississippi – with trees, and a paddle steamer (made of cardboard)*

Costumes and Props Box
- ✓ *t-shirts, shorts and straw hats for the boys*
- ✓ *raggy clothes and chains for Jim*
- ✓ *some kitchen equipment: a mixing bowl and wooden spoon, scrubbing brush, etc.*
- ✓ *a raft, made with either wood or card*
- ✓ *teapot and teacups*

Sound and Lighting
- ✓ *tape of a river sound*
- ✓ *coloured lights for the final song and dance*

Other Considerations
- ✓ *you could get away with just one set: the banks of the Mississippi*
- ✓ *'slavery' and 'freedom' are good school topics*

Peter Pan and Friends

In Brief

Wendy and her two brothers John and Michael love reading bedtime stories about Peter Pan. Word gets out to Peter Pan himself who comes to sit on their windowsill to listen to the adventures. One night Peter asked the children to join him in Neverland, and after teaching them how to fly (with some practice and a sprinkle of fairy dust) whisks them off to a land of fun and adventure. They discover a land of fairies in treetops, mermaids swimming in a lagoon, and ships full of pirates.

J.M. Barrie created the fictional character of Peter Pan, which was first published under the title 'Peter Pan in Kensington Gardens' in 1906, and the play had premiered two years before under the title 'Peter Pan, or The Boy Who Wouldn't Grow Up'. He is 'stuck' at age 13 or 14, apparently because the author's older brother, David, died in a skating accident the day before his 14th Birthday – the family thought of David as forever a boy who 'wouldn't grow up'.

Peter's appearance is mostly left to the imagination of the reader, but his costume is more defined on stage and in film: a green tunic and tights, and a cap with a red feather, and green 'winkle-picker' shoes. He often plays the flute or a pipe which suggests his mythological origins. He has a 'beautiful smile', and has pointed ears, brown eyes, and light brown or red hair. Often on stage he is played by a petite-looking woman or girl.

As for Peter's personality, he is the stereotype of a boastful and careless boy, a symbol of a carefree and cocky childhood. Though selfish and self-centred, he is willing to put himself in danger to help his friends. His magical abilities are many: the ability to fly is the most important which he achieves using 'lovely wonderful thoughts' and fairy dust (the same dust that allows the children to fly from their room to Neverland). He is also a skilled swordsman, has good vision and hearing, and is skilled at mimicry (he can copy the voice of Captain Hook, for example). Other abilities include the ability to imagine things into existence, and a good ability to sense danger when it is near. And, of course, he has the ability to stay young, with unending youth!

So, who are his friends in Neverland, other than the three children (Wendy, John and Michael)? Here they are:

Tinker Bell: a fairy, Peter's loyal best friend whose dedication to him is everlasting;
Tiger Lily: a princess who is kidnapped and left on Marooners' Rock, to be rescued by Peter;
The Lost Boys: the boys were 'lost' by their parents after they fell out of their perambulators and then came to live in Neverland. Peter is their leader;
The Saltwater Crocodile: after peter cut off Captain Hook's right hand the crocodile ate it and got a taste for Hook's blood; it also swallowed a ticking clock that alerts Hook to its presence.

And his enemies:

Captain Hook: Pan's arch-enemy, who has a hook for a right hand (after Pan cut his right hand off); his two fears are the sight of his own blood, and the crocodile that continues to pursue him;
Mr. Smee: Hook's right-hand man, a rather clumsy pirate who seems incapable of capturing the Lost Boys; he prefers the pursuit of treasure.

These days you can visit the original Peter Pan statue in Kensington Gardens (adjoining Hyde Park) in London. It was erected overnight on 30th April 1912 as a May Day surprise for the children of London. Other than this statue, six other statues were cast from the mould which are in Brussels (Belgium), St. Johns (Canada), Camden (USA), Perth (Australia), Liverpool (UK) and Toronto (Canada). There are numerous other statues around the world too, though not from the original mould.

It is said that Wendy, John and Michael never forgot Neverland, even after they grew up.

Play: Journey to Neverland

Characters

Peter Pan
Wendy
John
Michael
Tinker Bell
The Crocodile
Captain Hook

Setting

Neverland: trees with fairies, a lagoon with mermaids, a pirate ship.

Script

Narrator: Once upon a time there were three children: Wendy, John and Michael. These children loved stories, especially bedtime stories. Let's join them for a fantastic adventure!

Scene 1: The Childrens' Bedroom

Wendy: Let's read a story.
John: Which story?
Michael: How about Peter Pan?
Wendy: Yeah! Good idea! There's a great story in this book. *(she takes the story book)* Here's a very special Peter Pan story.
Peter: *(he appears)* Hello, children! I'm Peter Pan. I've come to take you to Neverland!

Wendy: Wow! Really?
John: Amazing!
Michael: Let's go!
(they fly out of the window)

Scene 2: Neverland

Peter: Here we are in Neverland. Welcome! Let me show you around.
Wendy: Thanks, Peter.
Peter: Here are the multi-coloured trees, here are the mermaids, here is the magic stone, and here is the pirate ship... oh, no!
Wendy: What's wrong?
Peter: It's the pirate ship! That means the bad and wicked Captain Hook is nearby!
Hook: Ha ha! That's right! I'm here to capture you, little Pan, and your three pesky friends!
Peter: Run!
(they run away from Captain Hook, but he runs after them)
Hook: Ha ha! I've caught you! I will take you to my ship and you will never be free!

Scene 3: Captain Hook's Ship

John: Oh, no, what are we going to do?
Michael: Oh my goodness! What will Hook do with us?
Wendy: Don't worry, Peter Pan will save us.
Peter: I'm sorry, Wendy, but Captain Hook took my magic dust. I can't save you.
(suddenly...)
Tinker Bell: I am Tinker Bell, and I will save you!
Peter: Oh, Tinker Bell, can you really save us?

Tinker Bell: Yes, I still have lots of magic dust. *(she throws some magic dust)* Abracadabra! Run!

(they run)

Hook: Hey! You horrible little children! Come back!

Peter: No way! Goodbye, Hook!

Wendy: Bye!

John: Bye!

Michael: Bye!

Peter: And don't forget to look behind you!

Hook: What?

Peter: Behind you!

(Captain Hook looks behind him)

Crocodile: tick, tock, tick, tock, I will eat captain Hook!

Hook: On no! Run!

Crocodile: Tick, tock, tick, tock!

(the crocodile chases Hook off the stage)

Scene 4: The Children's Bedroom

Wendy: Wow, what an adventure.

John: Yes, it was very exciting.

Michael: It was amazing.

Peter: I'm glad we escaped from that dreadful Captain Hook. Thank you Tinker Bell.

Tinker Bell: You're welcome, Peter. I'd do anything for you!

Peter: It's time to go now. Goodbye, children.

Children: Goodbye!

(Peter Pan and Tinker Bell fly out of the window)

Wendy: Let's go to sleep now.

(the children go to sleep)

(All actors take a bow)

Director's Corner

Peter Pan is a fantasy story, so they say, so a lot of imaginative and 'unreal' things can happen: flying children, magic dust, and the like. This is a great play for fancy costume, not only for Peter, but also for captain Hook, the mermaids, or the crocodile. The most dramatic moment is when Hook chases the children around the stage.

The Set
- ✓ *the children's bedroom*
- ✓ *neverland, and the pirate ship*

Costumes and Props Box
- ✓ *green clothes and hat for Peter*
- ✓ *pirate's clothes for Hook*
- ✓ *casual clothes (bed clothes?) for the children*
- ✓ *crocodile mask*
- ✓ *magic dust – sand*

Sound and Lighting
- ✓ *tape of ticking clock sound*
- ✓ *a flash of light for when Tinker Bell appears*

Other Considerations
- ✓ *the moral is that you can overcome evil if you believe in magic*
- ✓ *don't use a real crocodile ;-)*

Charlie and the Chocolate Factory

In Wonka's words...

Hello my darlings! I'm Willy Wonka. I own the largest, best, most wonderful chocolate factory in the whole wide world! Or at least I used to, until I became too old to run the factory. I needed someone young to take over. I have no darling children of my own, you see. I devised a 'golden ticket' competition – some of my chocolate bars had a golden ticket hidden in them. The winning little darlings came to my factory. They were an odd bunch. Let me tell you about them in turn...

First was the delightful Violet Beauregarde. Delightful? Ha! The only thing delightful about this pushy little horror was that she visited my factory! She has a competitive spirit and especially when chewing gum! And that loud-mannered tomboy was even mean to dear little Charlie, calling him a 'loser'. Ironic, isn't it?

Her bad manners were here downfall, alongside her disobedience: I warned her most strongly not to eat my super gum that replicates a 3-course dinner, but did she listen? Ha! It was her own fault, that gum was not ready for human consumption. That last blueberry pie stage was (and I think still is) defective, and Violet dear turned herself into a giant blue blueberry! What a sight as she was rolled to the Juicing Room! It happens every time. They all become blueberries.

Then there was the memorable Veruca Salt. Memorable for the wrong reasons! She was an only child whose parents spoiled her like there was no tomorrow. She could not take 'no' for an answer, a greedy little girl who wanted everything she didn't have. Her motto was "I want, I want, I want" and she used some loud and immature behaviour to try and get this. She had no intention of losing an argument: when I told her strongly that she couldn't have one of my special squirrels, her response was simply to grab one as if it were hers! Well, the squirrels didn't like that one bit, decided she was a 'bad nut' (or 'bad egg' if you prefer), and sent her down the rubbish chute. That was the last we saw (or heard) of her!

Let me see, the next brute was Mike Teavee, more interested in television and video games than the factory, me, or anyone else but himself! Well, he was another one to ignore the words of the great Willy Wonka! In the Television Chocolate Room we saw an amazing giant chocolate bar being sent to TV, and you know that little brat wanted to do the same with himself! I tried to stop him, honestly I did, but it was rather funny to see a really small Mike Teavee stuck inside a TV screen. "Get me out of here!" he cried in his new-found squeaky voice. Can you believe it?

Then came Augustus Gloop, a "great big greedy nincompoop" as my Oompa-Loompas called him. That chubby thing certainly enjoyed his chocolate. His mother was so proud of him, claiming that the bigger he got, the more of him there was to love! Did he meet a sticky end! We were all in the Chocolate Room, you see, and I let the dear children try anything they wanted to eat – candy flowers, fudge trees, and the like. Well, little, er, big Augustus ran straight for the lake of melted chocolate but in his endeavour leant too far out and, oh ha ha, fell into the chocolate! He got sucked up the chocolate extraction pipe, at first blocking the pipe, then after a shove from my Oompa-Loompas made his sticky way through a maze of pipes to the Fudge Room. I believe he was 'de-fudged'.

Finally, last but not least my darlings, came young Charlie Bucket, the eventual winner. What a fine little fellow, so virtuous and pure! Though very poor, he never complained, and only spoke when spoken to. Oh, well, I felt sorry I guess, you know, walking to school in the cold everyday, looking after his bedridden grandparents, and the rest of it. But behind the humble exterior I saw an inner strength and courage; he faced (and still faces) the challenges and mysteries of the factory with the same bravery that he employed to overcome the problems of his everyday life. That's why I chose him to take over my glorious factory!

And there you have it, my lovely friends! If you do happen to come to Charlie's chocolate factory all I can suggest is: don't eat the blueberry gum, don't ask for a pet squirrel, don't send yourself into a television, and don't try to drink the chocolate river! Enjoy your sugary treats, my lovelies, and goodbye!

Play: How To Win A Chocolate Factory Competition

Characters

Charlie
Grandpa
Willy Wonka
Violet
Veruca
Mike
Augustus

Setting

Mr. Wonka's chocolate factory: pipes, vats and machines

Script

Charlie: Hi, I'm Charlie Bucket, and I'm gonna tell you how to win a chocolate factory competition. It's quite easy, really. The way to do it is to look at how NOT to win a chocolate factory competition. Let me demonstrate: here's our first example, Violet Beauregarde.

Violet: Yummy yummy gum, I love gum! Willy, give me some blueberry gum!
Willy: Well, Violet darling, the blueberry gum isn't ready yet.

Violet: Isn't ready yet? It looks ready to me. Give it to me! *(she grabs the gum)*
Willy: Oh, no, don't…
Violet: what's happening? I'm getting bigger and I'm turning blue! I'm turning into a blueberry!
Willy: Oh, well, I did warn you. Take her to be squeezed.

Charlie: Hmmm. Blueberry pie will never taste the same again. Well, now to our second example, Veruca Salt.

Veruca: I want, I want, I want. Mr. Wonka, give me one of your special squirrels.
Willy: Veruca, my little dear, the squirrels are not to be given away.
Veruca: Huff! I want, I want, I want! I will have one of those pesky squirrels!
Willy: Oh, no, don't…
Veruca: Come here, you little animal, come here… *(she falls into the rubbish chute)* Oh no! Ahhhhhhh!
Willy: Oh, dear, well I did warn her, but now she's just rubbish in the rubbish chute. Hmmm…

Charlie: She was a bad nut. OK, on to our next example, dear little Mike Teavee.

Mike: Give me video games! Give me computer games! Shoot! Shoot! Shoot! Pow!
Willy: Oh, how delightful. Mike, dear, do you like TV?
Mike: TV? Yeah! Shoot! Shoot! Pow!
Willy: How about this special TV?
Mike: Yeah! Look, I'm inside the TV! I'm on TV!

Willy: Oh, no, don't...
Mike: Oh no, I'm stuck!
Willy: Stuck on TV. Never mind.

Charlie: He always wanted to be on TV, haha! Time now for our last example of how NOT to win a chocolate factory competition, Augustus Gloop.

Augustus: Yummy! Chocolate! Chocolate everywhere!
Willy: Darling, be careful, the chocolate river is dangerous.
Augustus: Dangerous? Chocolate? Never! I will eat ALL the chocolate in this river!
Willy: Oh, no, don't...
Augustus: *(he falls in)* My goodness! I can't swim! Mr. Wonka, help me! Ahhhhh...
Willy: There he goes, into the chocolate pipes. Goodbye!

Charlie: There you have it; how NOT to win a chocolate factory competition. How do you win? Make sure your name is Charlie Bucket, don't eat the blueberry gum, don't ask for a pet squirrel, don't send yourself into a television, and don't try to drink the chocolate river! Bye!

(All actors take a bow)

Director's Corner

This is such a fun play with a lot of action involved: getting bigger and becoming a blueberry, and going down the rubbish chute to name but two. I'm really leaving how you present this to your imagination (and budget), as long as you keep the humour.

The Set
- ✓ *the various parts of a chocolate factory; a chocolate river, rubbish chute, giant TV screen, a blueberry room.*

Costumes and Props Box
- ✓ *Wonka has a top hat, tail coat, and cane*
- ✓ *Charlie's clothes are raggy and brown*
- ✓ *the children's clothes are smart and well-presented*

Sound and Lighting
- ✓ *'gurgling' chocolate sound*
- ✓ *'zap' and 'twinkle' sound effects, as events happen*

Other Considerations
- ✓ *the story contrasts the angelic Charlie with the other 'beastly' children*
- ✓ *don't use real chocolate ;-)*

Peter the Wild Boy

In Brief

Back in 1726 King George I of England was hosting a dinner party in the German town of Hamelin (in the province of Hanover) when some local folks presented a young boy who had been found in the Hertswold Forest. The boy was named 'Peter' and had the nickname 'Peter the Wild Boy'.

The boy was just eleven or twelve years old and found naked, filthy, badly sun-burned, and walking on all fours. Despite his straggly appearance he was very agile, able to move about very quickly and climb trees with ease. Speculation was that he had been abandoned and brought up by a wild pig, wolf or bear.

Caroline, Princess of Wales, took an interest in Peter's welfare and had him brought back to England where he lived at Kensington Palace. He was very popular with the Royal Court and though the King treated him kindly, he was seen as a strange and entertaining 'human pet'.

In London he learned to walk upright, and was seen to express emotions just like any other human. He was a gentle soul with a jovial nature who everyone adored. But all attempts to civilise him failed. He ate with his hands, disliked wearing clothes, and could not be taught to speak. Furthermore he would not sleep in his bed, but preferred to curl up on the floor in the corner of his room.

After a time he was moved to Northchurch in Hertfordshire under the care of Mrs. Titchbourn (a servant in the Royal House). Peter had a succession of carers and finally settled at a farmhouse named 'Broadway' where he lived with his new carer, Farmer Brill, until his death in 1785.

So what, if anything, was medically wrong with Peter? It was found that he had a rare genetic condition known as Pitt-Hopkins Syndrome, with characteristics including short stature, curly hair, 'cupid's bow' moth, learning and developmental difficulties, and inability to develop speech. The genetic condition was only identified in 1978.

Peter was apparently capable of understanding what was said, but he himself could only say the words 'Peter' and 'King George'. In later years he had a teacher, Mr. Braidwood, who specialised in teaching people with disabilities. He was able to teach Peter a few simple words that allowed him to answer simple questions. When asked who his father was he replied "King George".

These days you can find several reminders of Peter the Wild Boy. In the graveyard of St. Mary's Church in Northchurch is his gravestone. It was given Grade II listing in 2013. In 2007 a blue plaque was placed at the Wild Man Pub in Bedford street, Norwich. The Museum of Norwich has a small display. His collar, used to identify him should he get lost, is kept at Berkhamstead School in the Chilterns. Perhaps most accessible is a visit to Kensington Palace in London.

Play: Peter the Wild Boy

Characters

Peter
King George
Caroline (Princess of Wales)
Teacher
Doctor
Farmer Brill

Setting

Kensington Palace, a fine decorated 'court' room.

Script

King: Hello. What's your name?
Peter: Peter. P-P-Peter.
King: Where are you from?
Peter: Peter. P-P-Peter. I'm a wild boy.
King: A wild boy?
Caroline: Oh, daddy! Can we take him to England? Can I have him as a pet? Please!
King: OK, Caroline. What do you think, Peter?
Peter: King George! England! Yes!

(they go to England)

Caroline: Sit with us to eat, Peter.
King: Yes, sit with us to eat, Peter.
Peter: Yes, King George, yes! *(he starts to eat with his fingers and is very messy)*
Caroline: Use a knife and fork, Peter. Eat!
Peter: Yes, eat! *(he continues to eat with his fingers)*
King: Oh, Peter! You are very messy. You must eat with a knife and fork.
Peter; Yes, eat Peter, eat!
King: Let's ask the teacher, the doctor, and Farmer Brill.

(the teacher walks in)

Teacher: Hello. What's your name?
Peter: Peter.
Teacher: Who is your father?
Peter: King George.
Teacher: What's your favourite animal?
Peter: Bow-wow.
Teacher: Oh, you mean 'dog'?
Peter: Yes, bow-wow. Dog.
King: What's wrong with Peter?
Teacher: He can't speak. He can't read. He can't write. But he *can* understand.
King: Can you understand, Peter?
Peter: Yes, King George. Yes!

(later...)

Doctor: Hello. What's your name?
Peter: Peter.

Doctor: Who is your father?
Peter: King George.
Doctor: Can you understand, Peter?
Peter: Yes, doctor. Yes!
King: What's wrong with Peter?
Doctor: He has Pitt-Hopkins Syndrome.
King: What's that?
Doctor: He has learning and development difficulties. He cannot speak
– only a few words. It is a genetic condition.
King: But he looks so happy.
Doctor: I think he is happy.

(later...)

Farmer Brill: Hello. What's your name?
Peter: Peter.
Farmer: Who is your father?
Peter: King George.
Farmer: Really? You are funny. Will you come to live on my farm and
look after my animals?
Peter: Yes, Farmer Brill. Yes!
King: Goodbye, Peter. Have a good time on the farm with farmer Brill
and the animals.
Caroline: Goodbye, Peter.
Peter: Yes, King George. Yes, Caroline. Yes! *(he turns to the audience
and winks)* Goodbye!

(All actors take a bow)

Director's Corner

It's a 'rags to riches' story and contrasts the uneducated and ill-mannered Peter with the King and others in 'polite' society. I'd keep the set very simple, in a regal and royal court (dining) room, though it's possible to have an additional scene in the woodland when Peter is 'found'.

The Set
- ✓ *royal portraits in gold frames*
- ✓ *a banquet (dining) table and chairs*

Costumes and Props Box
- ✓ *Peter wears raggy clothes*
- ✓ *the others wear fine and expensive clothes*
- ✓ *food and drink (plastic?)*
- ✓ *knives and forks*
- ✓ *a book for Peter to 'read'*

Sound and Lighting
- ✓ *tape of eating / banquet sounds*
- ✓ *royal 'trumpet' sound, for the King*

Other Considerations
- ✓ *Peter has a stutter and cannot speak properly*
- ✓ *do you think Peter really was dumb, or was he really very clever?*

Pablo Picasso

In Brief

Reputedly Picasso could draw before he could talk, and his early years show a great deal of maturity and complexity that precede his later adventures into cubism.

Born on 25th October 1881 in Malaga, Spain, Picasso's first word was not 'mummy' or 'daddy' as with most children, but 'piz' which is short for pencil in Spanish. His father was a painter, mostly of birds, and he started to teach Pablo in drawing techniques and oil painting from the age of 7. By the age of 8 he had produced his first painting 'Le Picador', of a man riding a horse in a bullfight. His first major painting followed when he was 15, 'First Communion', a portrait of his father, mother and younger sister kneeling before an altar.

In 1891 he moved with his family to northern Spain where he studied at the Instituto de Guarda; then in 1896 at an art school in Barcelona; and a year later he started at the Academia San Fernando in Madrid, but only lasted there a year as he preferred art and the real world as opposed to study. His first works were illustrated in a newspaper and exhibition in Barcelona in 1900. Later that year he first travelled to Paris, burning his own paintings during the cold winter to keep warm! Finally in 1904 he moved to Paris which was seen as the most cutting-edge city for artists.

Many of his works included children, and throughout his life Picasso did many portraits and drawings of children. He had four children of his own (Paulo, Maia, Claude and Paloma) and used them and his friends' children as models. For example:

First Communion (1896) – his first large-scale oil painting;
Child Holding a Dove (1901) – at the start of his 'blue period';
Mother and Child (1901) – with religious connotations, themes of religion and poverty;
Boy with a Pipe (1905) from his 'rose period', was sold at auction in 2004 for $104 million;
Two Acrobats with a Dog (1905) – showing harlequin, a significant motif in Picasso's work;
Horse with a Youth in Blue (1905-6) – watercolour and gouache;
Child with Flower (1945) – cubism, surrealism;
Claude Writing (1951) – represents Picasso himself, not writing but drawing;
Mother and Children with an Orange (1951) – abstract art;
Paloma en Bleu (1952) – Paloma means 'dove' in Spanish.

Picasso was very versatile with his techniques and used a variety of media: oil, watercolour, gouache and India ink. Each technique conveyed a particular meaning to the artwork. He liked to experiment and try out new ideas, and as time went on he helped us see the world in new ways. In particular, he has shown how closely colours are connected to human emotions, and how paintings can reflect not just the artist's emotional state, but also the state of society as a whole.

A couple of Picasso's quotes summarise his attitude to life and to art. The first is reminiscent of Peter Pan when he says "All children are artists. The problem is how to remain an artist once he grows up". The second refers to what he wanted to be when he grew up: "when I was a child my mother said to me, 'If you become a soldier, you'll be a general. If you become a monk you'll end up as the pope.'" He later said "Instead I became a painter and wound up as Picasso".

Play: How to Paint Like Picasso

Characters

Picasso
Artist 1 (Dali)
Artist 2 (Constable)
Artist 3 (Turner)
Artist 4 (Moore)
Judge

Setting

An art studio in Paris: easels, pots of paint and brushes, vases of flowers

Script

Judge: Hello, and welcome to our beautiful art studio in Paris! Today we're going to learn how to paint like Picasso. So, let's welcome the man himself, Pablo Picasso.
(audience claps and cheers)
Picasso: Buenos Dias! I am the magnificent Pablo Picasso, and I will teach four ordinary people to paint, before your very eyes!
Judge: Wow, Picasso, this will be something to watch. So let's meet our four ordinary people.
(the four people walk on)
Artist 1: Hello, my name's Dali and I'm an artist.
Artist 2: Hello, my name's Constable and I'm an artist.
Artist 3: Hello, my name's Turner and I'm an artist.

Artist 4: Hello, my name's Moore and I'm an artist.
Judge: Can any of you paint like Picasso?
(they all shake their heads 'no')
Judge: Then, let's begin. Picasso, what's the first technique you're going to show us?
Picasso: Ola, it is going to be experimentation with shapes and cubism...
Dali: I'll try this one.
Picasso: First draw a square, then a circle, then a triangle.
Dali: OK, here. *(he draws)* What is it?
Picasso: Ola, what is it? It's a human face!
Dali: Oh, yes!
Judge: Wow, that's amazing, Picasso. What's the next technique you're going to show us?
Picasso: Ola, it's going to be the use of oil and watercolour...
Constable: I'll try this one.
Picasso: Put the oil on the canvas like this, but put the watercolour on the canvas like this, up and down, left and right.
Constable: Like this? *(he paints)* Very nice, but what is it?
Picasso: Ola, they are trees!
Constable: Oh, yes!
Judge: Amazing, Picasso. What's next?
Picasso: Ola, we're going to look at relative shape and size, especially the human body...
Moore: I'll try this one.
Picasso: Here is the body, here are the arms, and here are the legs.
Moore: Where is the face? The head?
Picasso: The face? The head? I am Pablo Picasso, and my art does not need a face or a head.
Moore: Oh, yes, that's real art.
Judge: That's cool! What's your final technique? Is it going to be politics

in art?

Picasso: Ola, no, my final technique is the representation of life and death...

Turner: I'll try this one.

Picasso: Life is bright colours, yellow, orange, light green, red!

Turner: Like this? *(he paints)*

Picasso: Yes! And death is dark colours, brown, purple, black!

Turner: Like this? *(he paints)*

Picasso: Yes! Death! Oh, no, I don't feel well. I'm dying! *(he rolls on the floor)*

Judge: My goodness, that's realistic!

Picasso: No, I really am dying!

Judge: Really? Call the doctor! Too late!

Picasso: Drink to me, drink to my health, you know I can't drink any more *(he dies)* Ahhhh!

Judge: There we have it, ladies and gentlemen, now we know how to paint like Picasso.

(All actors take a bow)

Director's Corner

Here we are in an artist's studio in Paris, learning how to paint like Picasso. Each of the 'ordinary' people take it in turn to try a different technique, and they all appreciate the greatness of Picasso – who then dies with famous last words.

The Set
    ✓ *an artist's studio, with the Eiffel Tower in the background*

Costumes and Props Box
    ✓ *artist's capes and hats*
    ✓ *a colour mixing board and brushes*
    ✓ *easels and pots of brushes and paint*
    ✓ *four blank easels – one for each of the artists to paint or draw on*

Sound and Lighting
    ✓ *each of the four easels must be clearly visible to the audience and well-lit*

Other Considerations
    ✓ *try reproducing Spanish and French accents*
    ✓ *look on the internet for real examples of Picasso's work*

Mozart: Boy Genius

In Brief

As child prodigies go, Wolfgang Amadeus Mozart is a pretty good example. Not only could he play and compose music from a very early age, he was also very prolific writing over 600 musical works in his 35-year life.

Mozart was born on 27th January 1756 in Salzburg, Austria. At a young age he was heavily influenced by his father, Leopold, a well-known violinist and composer employed by the Archbishop of Salzburg. He was also influenced by his older sister, Nannerl, who also had a talent for music. As a child of three years he used to watch Nannerl intensely as she practiced the keyboard under instruction from their father. He used to mimic her playing and showed a strong understanding of chords, tone and tempo.

It was only a matter of time before Mozart himself started music lessons.

By the age of five he could play the violin and harpsichord with ease, and even write short musical pieces which his father wrote down for him. His father said that he played the keyboard "without fault and with great sensitivity".

By the age of six he was travelling and performing throughout Europe with his parents and sister. They performed in Munich, Prague, Paris, The Hague, and London. In London he performed for King George III, and furthermore met and played duets with Johann Christian Bach, son of

Johann Sebastian Bach.

He travelled to Italy with his father in 1769, aged 13. He heard music by many well-known Italian composers including Gregorio Allegri. Allegri had written a piece 'Miserere' for the Pope to be performed by a choir in the Sistine Chapel. No one was allowed to see the written music. But Mozart heard it just once and was able to write it all down from memory.

His first important opera, Idomeneo, was first performed in Munich in 1770.

He finally settled in Vienna in 1771, and in 1772 married Constanze Weber. In 1772 he wrote another very successful opera 'The Abduction from the Seraglio'. When the Emperor heard the opera he remarked that there were "too many notes" to which Mozart replied "Just as many as are necessary, Your Majesty".

His music is considered the very best of 'classical' style; he was the first composer to write music for the piano (which had only just become popular). He wrote every kind of music; symphony, opera, concerto, chamber music, piano sonatas, religious music, dances, serenades... the list goes on. Some famous compositions that are well-known today include 'Eine Kleine Nachtmusik', 'Turkish Rondo', 'Birdcatcher's Song' (from 'The Magic Flute'), and 'Ah vous drais-je, Maman' (Twinkle Twinkle Little Star). His good friend Joseph Haydn said "[he is] the greatest composer known to me... he has taste... and the most profound knowledge of composition".

But Mozart's life seemed to roller-coaster from financial stability to periods of debt, especially in the late 1780s. Early on in the decade Mozart and his family enjoyed a lavish lifestyle, lived in an exclusive apartment building, and sent their children to expensive schools. His opera 'Die Entfuhrung' was a great success and his concerts were very well attended and he had a 'unique' connection with his audiences. But further into the decade he fell into serious financial difficulties despite musical success. The low point was in 1788-99 when he suffered from depression. Thankfully by 1790 his musical productivity returned, and so did his success, for example 'The Magic Flute'. Though his finances improved again, his mental and physical health were deteriorating. His last (unfinished) work 'Requiem' (a mass for the dead) shows that he must have known he was ill. Finally on 5th December 1791 he died, probably from rheumatic fever, though the cause of death is uncertain.

There are many words to describe Mozart: vivid, prolific, talented, sophisticated, restless, complex, genius, to name but a few. However we describe him, he had a profound effect on the development of classical music, which extends to this day. And to quote the man himself: "Neither a lofty degree of intelligence nor imagination nor both together go to the making of genius. Love, love, love, that is the soul of genius".

Play: Speak to the Star: Mozart

Characters

Mozart
Interviewer
Leopold (Mozart's father)
Haydn (Mozart's friend)
Emperor Joseph II

Setting

A finely decorated opera house in Vienna.

Script

Interviewer: *(standing)* Hello, and welcome to 'Speak to the Star'. Tonight's guest is the well-known composer and musician, Wolfgang Amadeus Mozart.
(audience claps; Mozart walks in and sits down)
Mozart: Good evening.
Interviewer: Thank you for coming here tonight.
Mozart: No problem. It's a pleasure.
Interviewer: My first question is about your music. What kind of music do you write?
Mozart: Well, mostly I write symphony, opera, concerto, chamber music and piano sonatas.
Interviewer: And what's a symphony?

Mozart: Good question. A symphony used to be a short, simple piece of music used for entertainment, but I changed it into a longer piece, up to half an hour, with many musical instruments.

Interviewer: I hear that you work very hard. How many musical compositions have you written?

Mozart: I've written over 600.

Interviewer: And what are your best works?

Mozart: My favourite works are 'A Little Night Music', 'Turkish Rondo' and 'Birdcatcher's Song'.

Interviewer: Right. Time to bring in our next guest, Leopold, your father. Welcome.

Leopold: Good evening.

Interviewer: What do you think of your son's talent? You are his teacher, yes?

Leopold: Yes, I am his teacher.

Interviewer: Tell us about your son and student.

Leopold: He is very talented; he plays without fault and with great sensitivity. He is a very prolific writer.

Interviewer: OK. Let's bring in our next guest, Haydn.

Haydn: Good evening.

Interviewer: You and Mozart are good friends, yes?

Haydn: Yes. We write music together and we play in a string quartet together.

Interviewer: And what do you think of his musical talent?

Haydn: He is the greatest composer known to me. He has taste and the most profound knowledge of composition.

Interviewer: Good. Now our next guest, Emperor Joseph II. Good evening Your Majesty.

Emperor: Good evening.

Interviewer: What do you think about Mozart's operas?

Emperor: I think they are good, but they contain too many notes.
Interviewer: Too many notes? Mozart, what do you reply?
Mozart: I reply that there are just as many notes as are necessary.
Interviewer: That's a good answer. Now then, Mozart, they say you are a musical genius. What do you say to that?
Mozart: I say that neither a lofty degree of intelligence nor imagination nor both together go to the making of genius. Love, love, love, that is the soul of genius!
Interviewer: Well, that's all tonight on 'Speak to the Star'. I'll see you next week. Goodnight.
(the audience claps)

(All actors take a bow)

Director's Corner

Every guest on this talk show loves Mozart and sings his praises. You can really go to town with old-style costumes and large, wavy white wigs. Try starting and ending the play with some of Mozart's music.

The Set
- ✓ *the talk show is set in an old-style concert room, in an old house in Vienna, with large musical notes on the walls*

Costumes and Props Box
- ✓ *Mozart wears a big, white wig*
- ✓ *all are dressed formally and are flamboyant and fancy*
- ✓ *chairs for the host and guests*
- ✓ *some musical instruments*
- ✓ *sheets of music*

Sound and Lighting
- ✓ *tape of an extract from Mozart's work*

Other Considerations
- ✓ *for copyright reasons don't use more than a few seconds of Mozart's work*
- ✓ *what questions would you like to ask Mozart?*

Before the Beatles

In Brief

The Beatles are one of the biggest acts in music history, especially the song-writing partnership of John Lennon and Paul McCartney. But a lot happened in the few years prior to the formation of the Beatles, in particular a couple of bands that were the nursery for greater things to come. There are two main strands to the story: first, the Quarrymen fronted by John Lennon, and second Rory and the Hurricanes from where Ringo Starr came.

Back in 1957 John Lennon created the Quarrymen with a bunch of friends at Quarry Bank High School, Liverpool. Though the band's lineup was fairly fluid, their musical style was, at least at first, a musical style known as 'skiffle'. Skiffle originated in the US and had been popular there in the 20s, 30s and 40s. Now it had become popular with British teenagers with many boys starting their own groups — like the Quarrymen. It was popular because it didn't require great musical skills or expensive instruments. Early British skiffle was played by jazz musicians, the most successful (and emulated) being Lonnie Donegan.

Skiffle included a couple of homemade instruments alongside the more conventional banjo, guitar and drums. The 'washboard' was a percussion instrument, and could be played by strumming the ribbed metal surface of the board in a rhythmical way. The 'Tea-chest Bass' was made from a pole (probably a broomstick) placed into a tea chest; a chord was attached to the centre of the tea chest and to the pole, and plucking or strumming the chord made low base tones. The result of the ensemble was a rhythmic and animated home-grown sound.

This skiffle sound gradually faded away to be replaced by rock and roll.

The Quarrymen had various band members including Pete Shotton (washboard), Eric Griffiths (lead guitar), Rod Davis (banjo), Bill Smith (tea-chest bass) and Colin Hanton (drums). But of course the real moment came when John Lennon met Paul McCartney at the Woolton Village Fete on Saturday 6th July 1957. The official name of the event was the St. Peter's Church Rose Queen Garden Fete.

Lennon and his band first played on the back of a flatbed truck as the procession made its way through the streets. Later in the day the band moved to a fixed stage behind the church, and it was here that a young Paul McCartney arrived and was introduced to Lennon. They chatted, and Lennon was impressed by McCartney's knowledge of some new songs which included 'Twenty Flight Rock', 'Be-Bop-A-Lula' and a medley of Little Richard songs. Of course, McCartney was duly invited to join the band.

When George Harrison joined in 1959 at the tender age of 14, the groups sound moved noticeably away from skiffle and towards rock and roll.

The Quarrymen's first recording session was booked for 12th July 1958 at Phillips' Sound Recording Services in Liverpool. They recorded 'That'll Be The Day' and 'In Spite Of All The Danger' straight onto a 78rpm disc with the use of a single microphone in the middle of the room. In early 1960 they went back to the same studio to record Lennon's 'One After 909'. By March 1960 they had the name the Beatles and in 1962 signed with Parlophone, who took them to the top.

The other important strand 'before the Beatles' was Rory and the

Hurricanes, whose three members were Rory Storm (Alan Caldwell), Ty Brian, and a certain Ringo Starr. Originally the band was named 'Al Caldwell's Texans', then 'The Raving Texans' and finally Rory and the Hurricanes. Their first appearance was at the Mardi Gras Club in Liverpool on 29th March 1958. They also played at the Cavern Club in the days when it was a jazz club, but were fined by the owner for playing too much rock and roll. At the Kaiserkeller in Hamburg Rory and the Hurricanes were billed as the main group, *above* the Beatles!

So, where are they now? At least, where are the non-Beatle members now? The Quarrymen are still around. In 1994 and 1995 Davis and Lowe recorded the 'Open for Engagements' album, released in 1995. In 1997 the surviving members of the band reunited to perform at the 40th anniversary celebration of the Woolton Village Fete (Shotton, Davis, Garry, Griffiths and Hanton). They have since toured the UK, US, Germany and Japan, to name a few. Their musical style is distinctly un-Beatles, focusing instead on skiffle sounds and 50s rock and roll covers.

Ringo Starr is still going strong as a solo artist, but the fate of the other two members of Rory and the Hurricanes is less happy. Back in 1967 Ty Brian collapsed on stage and died of complications after an operation. He was only 26. Rory himself was found dead at his home in September 1972, perhaps due to an overdose of sleeping tablets.

All in all a lot happened in the years before the Beatles, but gradually the Fab Four came together, the final piece in place when Ringo joined in August 1962 – just in time for their first chart success 'Love Me Do' in late 1962.

The Quarrymen

Years Active: 1956-1960, 1994-present

Current Members:
Colin Hanton – drums
Rod Davis – guitar, vocals
Len Garry – vocals, guitar
John "Duff" Lowe – keyboards, vocals
Chas Newby – bass guitar

Former Members:
John Lennon – vocals, guitar
Eric Griffiths – guitar
Pete Shotton – washboard
Bill Smith – tea-chest bass
Nigel Walley – tea-chest bass, manager
Ivan Vaughan – tea-chest bass
Paul McCartney – vocals, guitar
George Harrison – guitar, vocals
Ken Brown – guitar
Stuart Sutcliffe – bass guitar

Albums:
'Open for Engagements' (1995)
'Get Back – Together' (1997)
'Songs We Remember' (2004)
'Grey Album' (2012)

Singles:
'In Spite Of All The Danger' (1958)
'That'll Be The Day' (1958)
'No 6'

Rory Storm and the Hurricanes

Years active: 1959-1967

Former Members:
Rory Storm (Alan Caldwell) vocals
Ringo Starr (Ritchie Starkey) drums
Ty O'Brien (Charles O'Brien) lead guitar
Johnny Byrne rhythm guitar
Lou Walters bass guitar

Albums:
'The Complete Works' (1994)
'Live at the Jive Hive March 1960' (2012)

Singles:
'Dr Feel Good' (1963)
'America' (1964)

Play: Before The Beatles

Characters

Narrator
John Lennon
Paul McCartney
Ringo Starr
Rory storm
Dick Rowe

Setting

Madame Tussauds, Woolton Village Fete, Decca Recording Studio

Script

Scene 1: Madame Tussauds, London, 2020

Narrator: I went to see Madame Tussauds waxworks in London. It has wax models of many famous people. My favourite was the Beatles. An old man came up to me – he looked familiar but I couldn't place him, but his voice had a familiar Liverpool accent. He started to speak.
Old Man: Do you like the Beatles? Yes? They were just a band, who made it very, very big.
Narrator: Really? Do you know about the Beatles?
Old Man: I knew them, you know.
Narrator: You knew them?
Old Man: Yes. But do you know the story of before the Beatles?

Narrator: No, I don't. His face looked poetic and his memory seemed bright. I asked him to go on.
Old Man: Let me take you down to the Woolton Village Fete in Liverpool, 1957...

Scene 2: Woolton Village Fete, 1957

John: Hello everybody, and welcome to Woolton Village Fete and we are the Quarrymen.
(audience claps and cheers)
John: Let's play that old skiffle song by Lonnie Donegan, 'My Old Man's A Dustman'. One, two, three four! (they play)
Paul: Hey, man, that's cool.
John: Thanks. Do you play?
Paul: Yeah, I play guitar.
John: What songs can you play?
Paul: Twenty Flight Rock, Be-Bop-A-Lula, and a Little Richard Medley.
(he plays)
John: Wow! That's cool, man! Will you join my band?
Paul: Sure, man!

Scene 3: The Cavern Club, Liverpool, 1959

John: Welcome to the Cavern Club, Liverpool. We're gonna start with an old number, Be-Bop-A-Lula.
(they start to sing)
Paul: Thank you very much. Our next song is one we wrote ourselves, it's called 'Hello Little Girl'.
(they start to sing)
Paul: Thank you very much. We're gonna take a short break.

John: Who's this?

Paul: This is George. He wants not join the band.

George: I can play guitar, man. Can I join the Quarrymen?

John: How old are you?

George: I'm nearly 15. Let me join, please! *(he demonstrates his guitar playing)*

John: OK, George. You're young but you play a mean guitar. You can join.

Scene 4: Kaiserkeller Club, Hamburg, 1960

Rory: (sings) We gotta whole lotta shakin' goin' on, we gotta whole lotta shakin' goin' on!

(audience claps and cheers)

Ty: That was great, Rory.

Ringo: Yeah, that was great!

Rory: Now we're gonna play a number by Buddy Holly, 'That'll Be The Day'. *(he sings, audience claps and cheers)*

Ty: That was great, Rory.

Ringo: Yeah, that was great! Who's on next?

Rory: Oh, that bunch of losers: the Beatles.

John: I heard you, Rory! We're not losers!

Paul: Yeah, we're not losers!

George: Yeah, we follow the sun!

Ringo: I'm joining the Beatles! Goodbye, Rory!

(they start to perform 'In Spite Of All The Danger')

Scene 5: Decca Recording Studio, London

Producer: *(in American accent)* Welcome to Decca, boys! My name's Dick Rowe. Who are you and what do you play?

John: I'm John, I play the guitar and sing. *(he plays the guitar and sings)*
Paul: I'm Paul, I play bass guitar. *(he plays bass guitar)*
George: I'm George, I play slide guitar. *(he plays slide guitar)*
Ringo: I'm Ringo, I play the drums. *(he plays the drums)*
Producer; What's your tune?
John: It's 'Love Me Do'.
(they perform the song, but half way through...)
Producer: OK, OK, stop! That's rubbish! You'll never make it big! Guitar groups are on their way out!
John: Hey, peace and love, man!
(they leave)

Scene 6: Madame Tussauds, London, 2020

Old Man: And that's the story before the Beatles.
Narrator: And the rest is history?
Old Man: Yeah, man, the rest is history. Can you imagine? *(he exits)*
Narrator: Wow! What a tale! And to think that he actually knew them! I looked at the waxworks. One of them looked familiar. Of course! It was the old man, but much, much younger. I turned to ask him 'Isn't that you?' but he was gone. Let me take you down, peace and love, imagine... it was John Lennon! No, surely, it couldn't have been...

(All actors take a bow)

Director's Corner

There are six scenes, but you needn't use a different set for each one. I'd recommend using either a set based on a club stage, or a recording studio (or both). Remember this was *before* the Beatles, so their fashion was very different: The Quarrymen often wore black leather jackets, while Rory and the Hurricanes wore colourful suits. Have fun!

The Set
- ✓ *a club stage, with musical notes on the walls*
- ✓ *a recording studio with microphones, musical instruments, and various recording equipment*

Costumes and Props Box
- ✓ *the Quarrymen wear black leather jackets and black trousers*
- ✓ *the Hurricanes wear colourful suits and ties*
- ✓ *various guitars*
- ✓ *a microphone*

Sound and Lighting
- ✓ *excerpts from various songs (Twenty Flight Rock, Be-Bop-A-lula, Love Me Do, etc)*
- ✓ *stage lighting and a glitter ball*

Other Considerations
- ✓ *just play short extracts from the songs for copyright reasons*
- ✓ *try to video your performance and sent it to Paul McCartney or Ringo Starr!*

References

How Dare You! The Greta Effect
- ❖ https://www.bbc.co.uk/newsround/49812183
- ❖ https://www.express.co.uk/news/world/1182871/Greta-Thunberg-who-is-Greta-Thunberg-parents-climate-change
- ❖ https://www.natgeokids.com/uk/kids-club/cool-kids/general-kids-club/greta-thunberg-facts/
- ❖ https://blogs.spectator.co.uk/2019/04/the-trouble-with-greta-thunberg
- ❖ https://www.thesun.co.uk/news/10765981/greta-thunberg-warns-world-leaders-speech-switzerland
- ❖ https://en.wikipedia.org/wiki/Greta_Thunberg
- ❖ https://www.yahoo.com/huffpost/mops-and-buckets-trump-climate-change-034911826.html

Sky Brown: Sky High
- ❖ https://www.bbc.com/sport/49704526
- ❖ https://www.bbc.com/sport/olympics/50726060
- ❖ https://hollywoodlife.com/2018/10/07/who-is-sky-brown-skateboarder/
- ❖ https://www.theguardian.com/sport/2019/dec/11/sky-brown-11-olympic-hopeful-britain-tokyo-2020-i-want-to-push-boundaries-for-girls
- ❖ https://wikibioage.com/sky-brown/
- ❖ https://en.wikipedia.org/wiki/Dancing_with_the_Stars:_Juniors

Coco Gauff: Cocomania
- ❖ https://www.bbc.com/sport/tennis/51253470
- ❖ https://www.telegraph.co.uk/tennis/2020/01/24/naomi-osaka-vs-coco-gauff-australian-open-2020-live-score-latest/
- ❖ https://www.tennisworldusa/tennis/news/Tennis_Stories/75368/coco-gauff-inspires-kids-on-first-day-of-school-work-hard-dream-big
- ❖ https://en.wikipedia.org/wiki/Coco_Gauff

Billie Eilish and Justin Bieber: Bad Guys
- ❖ https://www.biography.com/musician/justin-bieber
- ❖ https://www.imdb.com/name/nm3595501/

- https://www.nickiswift.com/144685/the-untold-truth-about-billie-eilish
- https://www.thefamouspeople.com/profiles/billie-eilish-42253.php
- https://en.wikipedia.org/wiki/Billie_Eilish
- https://en.wikipedia.org/wiki/Justin_Bieber

The Life and Death of Julius Caesar
- https://en.wikipedia.org/wiki/Julius_Caesar
- www.bbc.co.uk/history/historic_figures/caesar_julius.shtml
- http://www.ducksters.com/history/ancient_rome/julius_caesar.php
- https://www.britanica.com/biography/Julius-Caesar-Roman-ruler
- https://kids.kiddle.co/Julius_Caesar
- https://www.theschoolrun.com/homework-help/julius_caesar

Tutankhamun: Boy King
- https://www.biography.com/royalty/king-tut
- https://www.historyextra.com/period/ancient-egypt/8-things-you-probably-didnt-know-about-tutnkhamun
- https://www.history.com/topics/ancient-history/tutankhamun
- https://kids.kiddle.co/Tutankhamun
- https://londonist.com/london/museums-and-gallaeries/tutankhamun-treasures-coming-to-london-in-november
- https://en.wikipedia.org/wiki/Tutankhamun

Pocahontas: Powhatan Princess
- https://www.biography.com/historical-figure/pochahontas
- https://www.brittanica.com/biography/Pocahontas-Powhatan-princess
- https://www.ducksters.com/history/colonial_america/pocahontas.php
- https://www.imdb.com/title/tt0114148/
- https://www.smithsonianmag.com/history/true-story-pocahontas-180962649

Dick Whittington and His Cat
- https://www.bbc.co.uk/gloucestershire/content/articles/2005/06/16/about_dick_whittington_features_shtml
- https://www.its-behind-you.com/storydickwhittington.html
- https://www.purr-n-fur.org.uk/fabled/whittington.html
- https://www.worldstories.org.uk/stories/story/67-dick-whittington-and-

his-cat

Harry Potter and Friends
- ❖ https://www.beano.com/posts/harry-potter-which-harry-potter-character-are-you-personality-quiz
- ❖ https://harrypotter.fandom.com/wiki/Harry_Potter
- ❖ https://www.quora.com/How-would-you-describe-Harry-Potters-personality
- ❖ https://www.quora.com/What-characteristics-do-each-Ron-Harry-and-Hermione-bring-to-the-table
- ❖ https://www.quora.com/What-is-Hermione-s-personality
- ❖ https://www.quora.com/Why-is-Ron-represented-as-too-weak-in-comparison-with-Harry-and-Hermione
- ❖ https://en.wikipedia.org/wiki/Harry_Potter

Huckleberry Finn and Friends
- ❖ https://www.britannica.com/topic/Huckleberry-Finn-fictional-character
- ❖ https://www.imdb.com/title/tt0071634/plotsummary?ref_=tt_ov_pl
- ❖ https://www.sparknotes.com/lit/huckfinn
- ❖ https://en.wikipedia.org/wiki/Adventures_of_Huckleberry_Finn

Peter Pan and Friends
- ❖ www.bedtimestories.com/peter-pan-story-for-kids
- ❖ https://www.imdb.com/title/tt0046183
- ❖ https://kids.kiddle.co/Peter_Pan
- ❖ https://www.theguardian.com/childrens-books-site/2014/nov/25/top-10-things-peter-pan

Charlie and the Chocolate Factory
- ❖ https://charlieandthechocolatefactorythemusical.fandom.com/wiki/Augustus_Gloop
- ❖ https://www.roalddahl.com/roald-dahl/characters/children
- ❖ https://www.shmoop.com/charlie-chocolate-factory-book/veruca-salt.html
- ❖ https://www.sparknotes.com/lit/charlie/character/charlie-bucket/
- ❖ https://violetbeauregardefansite.weebly.com
- ❖ https://wonka.fandom.com/wiki/Violet_Beauregarde

Peter the Wild Boy

- ❖ https://www.bbc.com/news/magazine-14215171
- ❖ https://www.historicmysteries.com/peter-the-wild-boy
- ❖ https://www.historytoday.com/archive/peter-wild-boy
- ❖ https://thechilterns.blog/tag/peter-the-wild-boy/
- ❖ https://www.visitnorwich.co.uk/article/peter-the-wild-boy/
- ❖ https://en.wikipedia.org/wiki/Peter_the_Wild_Boy

Pablo Picasso

- ❖ https://answers.com/Q/How_many_children_did_Pablo_Picasso_have
- ❖ https://artsycraftsymom.com/top-10-pablo-picasso-projects-for-kids
- ❖ https://www.coolkidfacts.com/pablo-picasso
- ❖ https://kids.kiddle.co/Pablo_Picasso
- ❖ https://michelinewalker.com/2014/07/03/picassos-harlequin/
- ❖ https://www.periodpaper.com/collections/picasso-children-collection-1965
- ❖ primaryfacts.com/2091/pablo-picasso-facts-and-information
- ❖ https://www.tate.org.uk/kids/explore/who-is/who-pablo-picasso

Mozart: Boy Genius

- ❖ https://www.activityvillage.co.uk/mozart
- ❖ https://www.biography.com/musician/wolfgang-mozart
- ❖ https://kids.kiddle.co/Wolfgang_Amadeus_Mozart
- ❖ https://makingmusicfun,net/htm/f_mmf_music_library/hey-kids-meet-wolfgang-amadeus-mozart.php

Before the Beatles

- ❖ https://www.allmusic.com/artist/the-quarrymen-mn0000491444/biography
- ❖ https://www.discogs.com/artist/356120-The-Quarrymen
- ❖ https://www.last.fun/music/Rory+Storm+And+the+Hurricanes/+wiki
- ❖ https://www.last.fun/music/The+Quarrymen
- ❖ originalquarrymen.co.uk
- ❖ https://www.sweetwater.com/insync/tea-chest-bass

Barry Nicholson is an established educator with over twenty-five years' experience teaching adults, teens and children. Born and educated in the UK, he has lived and worked in Germany, Hong Kong, South Korea, Poland, Italy and Turkey. His first book was published in summer 2015, and this book adds to his strong literary archive.

From The Same Author

Fun Activities For Primary Children
Published February 2016   ISBN: 9780993243837
Planning a party, summer camp or extra-curricular class? Then you'll need some fun activities to liven things up and allow your children to participate and interact in a creative and informal atmosphere.

Poland In Play
Published April 2017   ISBN: 9780993243844
Poland is a fascinating and diverse country, and in this book you will find 16 stories from Poland's rich cultural history. Each story is accompanied by a play script designed for young learners.

Britain In Play
Published June 2017   ISBN: 9780993243851
Britain is a fascinating and diverse country, and in this book you will find 16 stories from Britain's rich cultural history. Each story is accompanied by a play script designed for young learners.

Animals In Play
Published January 2020   ISBN: 97809932468
Who doesn't love animals? Here you will find 16 animal stories, each accompanied by a play script that your children and teens will enjoy performing.